Grammar on the Go

QUICK & EASY BLACKBOARD ACTIVITIES

Victoria Holder

Addison-Wesley Publishing Company

A Publication of the World Language Division

Executive Editor: Elinor Chamas
Editorial: Nicole S. Cormen
Production: Kathy Sands Boehmer
Interior Design: Pageworks
Cover Design: Marshall Henrichs
Illustrations: Zheng Liu
Manufacturing: James W. Gibbons

DEDICATED TO
THE MEMORY OF
J. RAMON HEDBERG

ACKNOWLEDGMENTS

I would like to express special thanks to Loretta Nagel, who first tested my materials while teaching in Poland, to Nicole Cormen, a most patient, careful, and articulate editor, and to Patricia Porter for invaluable advice, guidance, and information about the publishing process. I would also like to express sincere appreciation to my illustrator, Zheng Liu, for his tireless, painstaking efforts at precision, as well as his total willingness and cooperation throughout. Finally, gratitude is due to my husband, Petr Brunclik, whose incredible understanding and enthusiastic support made it all possible.

ISBN: 0-201-59506-0
3 4 5 6 7 8 9 10 -CRS- 03 02 01 00

CONTENTS

INTRODUCTION

WHY THIS BOOK IS DIFFERENT

Grammar on the Go is a collection of contextualized grammar activities intended as supplemental practice for discrete grammar points in intermediate and advanced ESL or EFL classes. Four convenient distinguishing features characterize these activities:

1. They require no duplication of any kind. Blackboards (the more the better), scrap paper, and a box of straight pins are the only materials necessary for any activity in this book.

2. They require minimal preparation on the part of the instructor. A simple reading of the activity, and one to three minutes of writing or sketching on the blackboard immediately preceding the activity, are the maximum extent of preparation you will need.

3. All activities that require visual aids include simple but attractive drawings that easily can be copied onto the blackboard by any instructor, regardless of artistic skill.

4. A serious attempt has been made to make every activity appropriate for students in most settings around the world, whether ESL or EFL, from teenagers to adults. The activities do not require extensive knowledge of Western culture; they do not require that students all speak the same native language, nor that they all speak different languages or come from a variety of cultures.

THE ACTIVITIES

Type and Purpose

The activities contained in this book are primarily interactive pair and group work, with some whole-class arrangements. They range from relatively simple and straightforward substitution activities to more complex exchanges involving planning, problem solving, creative description, hypothesizing, and discussion. They are intended for accuracy practice—to teach rather than to test—and include ample suggested models. Most activities, however, can be revised to evaluate the students' control of a grammar point by limiting or eliminating some of the modeling.

The activities are also designed to provide oral practice, although most conclude with some form of blackboard writing by the students in order to verify accuracy and achieve closure. Most activities can be expanded to include larger individual writing assignments, if desired, in these **Accountability** sections (described ahead).

Level and Length

The activities in this book are not categorized according to level or length, because they all are appropriate for both intermediate and advanced students. The amount of time required will be determined largely by the level of your class. Intermediate students will require more instruction and explanation time, as well as more time to carry out the activity—in some cases up to 25 minutes—than more advanced classes, who might need as little as 15 minutes for the same activity. In fact, the oral nature of the instructions and tasks puts tremendous responsibility on the students, who can move through the activities only by talking. It is essential, then, that you give the instructions slowly and clearly, using the blackboard for as much modeling as necessary, especially with intermediate students. Once the students have begun the activity, it is helpful to circulate and be on the lookout for anyone who needs further explanation or encouragement.

In many cases, the grammar point itself will determine the level and the length of the activity. For example, the future perfect tense is likelier to be worked on at more advanced levels. In addition, review of a previously taught grammar point in an advanced class will usually go faster than will practice of a new grammar point in an intermediate class.

Organization

For quick reference and implementation, each activity is organized as follows:

Theme states the topic or content area of the activity, and, in parentheses, whether the activity asks students to use their imaginations or to exchange real information. Where appropriate, it also indicates if role-play or pantomime are involved.

Group size suggests the number of students who should work together, or whether the whole class works as one unit and/or as individuals on a one-on-one basis.

Goal defines the final task to be expected of the students. In most cases, this task will be performed during the **Accountability** stage.

Materials identifies what items, if any, you will need for the activity *besides* the blackboard, such as scrap paper and straight pins.

Numbered steps outline the procedure for each activity and begin with what goes on the blackboard. The blackboard material has been selected carefully for appropriateness and interest. You are welcome to adapt it for your own class (for example, to review more pertinent vocabulary), but any changes must maintain the logic of the activity in order to prevent confusion or complications in the students' responses. Please note that any text in parentheses is for your information and is not intended to be written on the blackboard.

The boxed instructions are meant to be given to the students and may be presented word for word. Here, as throughout the activity, the text in parentheses provides suggestions or clarifications for you, the instructor.

Accountability describes an appropriate paperless way to check on the students' accuracy during each activity. During this stage, the students report to the class or group and/or write on the blackboard. The precise format can be varied according to your type of class and the goal of the day's lesson. For example, in a large class, reporting to a group might go more smoothly than reporting to the whole class, while in a smaller class, reporting back to the entire class might be easier, more fun, and more informative.

Variation proposes specific ways to alter the activity. You also may want to record here your own ideas for variations, as well as unintended workable variations that emerge in class as you conduct the activity.

Drawings

The drawings in this book are designed to be copied easily. A few tips about how to approach them:

- Start from the top. For example, if there is a hat, start with the hat.

- Draw the whole circle for the head first, when drawing a person.

- Start with the nose when you draw a face.

- Draw a child's nose lower on the face than an adult's nose.

- If there is furniture, such as a chair, draw it last.

Versatility and Expansion

Just as the **Accountability** sections of many of the activities could be considered interchangeable, many of the activities themselves are also adaptable for practicing other grammar points. For example, the past-perfect puppy activity on page 49 adapts easily to the future perfect tense by changing "What had happened when . . ." to "What will have happened by the time . . ." Similarly, the schedule for next week on page 41 can be changed to last week to practice the past continuous tense instead of the future continuous.

While the primary inspiration for this book has always been to save paper (and, ultimately, trees), the activities here should also serve to save time and to inspire you to create your own activities by adapting, expanding, or transforming these ideas into others even more appropriate to your style, your needs, and your students. The easily-copied drawings should increase confidence in using blackboard art by practicing the simple models for recognizable objects and people. On the whole, this book should be considered not just as a collection of activities, but also as a springboard for your imagination and a blueprint for your own quick, paper-free, personalized activities. Have fun teaching grammar "on the go!"

COUNT / NON-COUNT NOUNS

Theme: Objects and people found in specific places (Imagination)

Group Size: Three to four students

Goal: Think of as many count and non-count items as possible found in various specific places.

1. Write on the blackboard:

   (Write each word at the top of the blackboard so that the students can make lists underneath. Each word represents the title of a category.)

A FOOD STORE (OR MARKET)	A BUS (OR TRAIN) STATION	A SHOE FACTORY	THE OCEAN
	noise		

A LIBRARY	AN OFFICE	A PARK	THE MOUNTAINS	ANOTHER PLANET
bookshelves	a desk			

2. Give each group the following instructions:

> Think of all the different things you might find in each place, and write them on the blackboard. Write *a* or *an* before singular count nouns, but write nothing in front of plural count and non-count nouns. After you have thought of several items for a specific category (place), have one member of your group write them on the blackboard while the rest of you continue to think of items for another category. If another group has already written your idea on the blackboard, you do not need to write it again. I have written some sample answers already.

Accountability: When all categories have several items listed underneath, you can go over what the groups have written on the blackboard and correct any errors.

Variation: With more advanced groups, or to make this a vocabulary exercise, you could use much more specific locations as categories, such as a bike shop, an opera house, an attic, and so on.

                  You also could make this activity into a competition by giving each group a number, and asking each group to identify all its entries on the blackboard by writing its number in parentheses. The group with the most entries on the blackboard wins.

COUNT / NON-COUNT NOUNS

Theme: Objects, people, places, and events (Imagination)

Group Size: Pairs

Goal: Guess a place or an event according to what a partner says he or she sees there.

1. Write on the blackboard:

Count
a lot of/many
a few
some
(any number)

Non-Count
a lot of
a little
some

2. Tell the class that when the activity begins, each student will be working with a partner. One partner will be facing you, the teacher, while the other partner will be facing the opposite direction, unable to see the teacher or the front blackboard. Demonstrate with a pair of students the exact position you want the pairs to take.

3. Write the word *beach* on the blackboard. Tell the students that you will be writing the names of different places, one at a time, on the blackboard during this activity. The student who cannot see the blackboard will try to guess each place according to the information his or her partner gives.

4. Explain to the class that the partner who can see the blackboard will tell the one who cannot see it some of the things that a person might see in such a place. For example, for *beach*, a student might say, *I see some sand.* or *I see many people in the water.* For each thing that the students see, they should use one of the words on the blackboard before the noun to show that they know whether it is count or non-count.

5. Have the students get into their positions as pairs, with one partner who can see you and one partner who cannot. Erase *beach* and write a new word on the blackboard from the following list:

PLACES	EVENTS
farm	party
big city	dance
small village	play
market or store	concert
school or university	movie

PLACES	EVENTS
ski area	wedding
museum	holiday or festival (specify)
village square or center	trial
stadium	sports event
hotel	vacation
movie theater	exposition
large apartment building	other local event or tradition (specify)
library	
forest	
concert hall	
courtroom	

6. Give each pair the following instructions:

> Those of you who can see the blackboard, tell your partner what you see in this place—people, buildings, machines, plants and animals, and so on. Partners, listen carefully. As soon as you think you know what the place is, quietly tell your talking partner. If your guess is correct, raise your hand. You have won the round.
>
> Each time someone guesses the place, I will change the word on the black-board. After several rounds, exchange roles.

Accountability: After each place is guessed, ask the listening partner to tell the class what the talking partner said that made it clear.

COUNT / NON-COUNT NOUNS

Theme: Picture on an artist's canvas (Imagination)

Group Size: Two to four very large groups, depending on the layout of your room and the amount of blackboard space

Goal: Get a student at the blackboard to complete a simple picture according to the group's instructions.

1. Put on the blackboard:

   a little

   a lot of

   a small amount of

   a little bit of

   many

2. Tell the class the following:

   > This is Gilbert. He is a painter, and he is going to paint some pictures for you. I will be drawing for Gilbert. You will tell me what to put in each picture—trees, people, buildings, cars, and so on. I will ask you how much or how many of each item to put in the picture; then I will draw it.
   >
   >   Now tell me what to put in the picture.

3. As each student suggests an item, ask how many or how much of it to put in the picture before you draw it. For example, if a student suggests a hill, ask *How many hills?* As the students reply, you may want to point to the list of expressions on the blackboard and review which ones are for count, and which ones are for non-count. Remind the students that they can always use a number for count nouns. Complete the picture.

4. Arrange the class in large groups, either standing or sitting, around separate sections of the blackboard. Quickly sketch a blank canvas (but no Gilbert) for each group. Have a student volunteer be the artist for each group.

5. Give each group the following instructions:

   > Tell your artist what you want in your group's picture. Before drawing anything, the artist should ask how much or how many of it to draw. Use the expressions on the blackboard, or a number, to answer. Unless your artist uses *much* or *many* correctly, do not tell him or her how much or how many to draw.

Accountability: When all of the pictures are done, have the students ask and answer questions about them.

ARTICLES

Theme: Familiar objects (Imagination)

Group Size: Whole class

Goal: Erase all the student-drawn objects from blackboard, one at a time.

1. Give the class the following instructions:

> Each person in the class should come to the blackboard and draw one, two, or three pictures of the same object. For example, you could draw one chair, two boxes, three faces, and so on. If you draw two boxes, the boxes should look the same. If you draw three faces, all three faces should look the same. Keep your pictures very simple. Look at what other people are drawing and do not draw an object that someone else is drawing.

If the class is small, the drawing can be done all at once, or in two or three shifts. In a large class, it can be done at the very beginning of class as the students come in. If there is too little time for students to draw, you may want to draw the objects yourself ahead of time, or just write words to represent the objects.

2. As the students finish drawing, have them sit down. A sample blackboard might look as follows:

3. Give the class these further instructions:

> We are now going to erase the blackboard completely, but one picture at a time. Each of you should speak several times. Choose any picture on the board and tell me to erase it. But remember, if there is more than one picture of the same object, you must use _a_; if there is only one picture, or if it is the last one, use _the_. For example, you would say, _Please erase a̲ cup_, but _Please erase t̲h̲e̲ ball_.

Accountability: Do not erase a picture unless the article is correctly used.

Variation: You may want to have the students practice the definite article in specific contexts. For example, have the students vary the sizes of the objects in each set. They can then give commands such as, _Please erase the tallest tree._ Or, have the students refer to the objects by their position: _the right tree, the middle tree,_ and so on.

    You also may wish to use a different command from _Erase the . . .,_ such as _Take away . . ., I don't like . . .,_ or encourage free variation of commands.

ARTICLES

Theme: Familiar objects (Real information exchange)

Group Size: Pairs

Goal: Find out about objects familiar to each partner.

1. Write on the blackboard:

   A. We have $\left\{\begin{array}{c}\text{windows}\\\text{a desk}\\\text{chalk}\end{array}\right\}$ in the classroom.

   B. What color $\left\{\begin{array}{c}\text{is}\\\text{are}\end{array}\right\}$ the_____?

       How $\left\{\begin{array}{c}\text{big}\\\text{long}\\\text{old}\end{array}\right\}$ $\left\{\begin{array}{c}\text{is}\\\text{are}\end{array}\right\}$ the _____?

2. Tell the students to look around the classroom and name something in the room, using model A on the blackboard. For example, a student might say, *We have books in the classroom.*

3. Ask that student a question according to model B on the blackboard, such as *What color are the books?* Allow the student to answer.

4. Write three new sample statements and questions on the blackboard, one for each of these three categories: singular count-noun, plural count-noun, non-count noun. Say the sentences, emphasizing each article or noting its absence, as in this example:

We have <u>a</u> desk.   What color is <u>the</u> desk?

We have chairs.   How big are <u>the</u> chairs?

We have paper.   What color is <u>the</u> paper?

5. Give each pair the following instructions:

> Tell your partner about objects in one of the following places: your whole house or apartment (or just your kitchen or your own room), your purse or pocket, or your hometown. Your partner should then ask you an appropriate question about each item. Try to use a variety of nouns—as well as singular and plural count nouns. After you have talked about eight to ten objects, exchange roles.

Accountability: Circulate during the practice, listening to each pair do at least one exchange.

ARTICLES

Theme: Household objects and people (Imagination)

Group Size: Whole class

Goal: Place and move objects and people in a house.

1. Put on the blackboard:

bedrooms

living room (right
dining room (left)

attic

2. Give the class the following instructions:

> Tell me what to put in the different rooms of the house. I will draw and move things for you. After some things are already in the house, you may tell me what to put in, on, next to, or under them. If you want, you can tell me to move an object that someone else has put in the house. You may also tell me to put people in the house, and then say what the person is wearing or holding.
>
> Remember to use *a* the first time you mention an object or person, and *the* every time after that. For example, if one student says, *Put a table in the middle bedroom*, another student can say, *Put a glass on the table*, or *Move the table to the dining room.*

Accountability: Do not draw the item in the house if the article is not used correctly.

Variation: Divide the students into pairs. On scraps of paper, have each partner draw an empty house and take turns dictating items for the other partner to draw.

If a house is inappropriate or uninteresting for your class, you might want to use a landscape, a store, a school, or even a street scene. Use whatever context is easily recognized and can be drawn by you and your students.

SUBJECT-VERB AGREEMENT

Theme: Likes and dislikes (Real information exchange)

Group Size: Three students

Goal: Exchange opinions about specific items.

1. Write on the blackboard:

dogs	rice	salad	opera
fish	coffee	milk	swimming
cats	(a holiday)	(a famous person known to the whole class)	

   I like cats. X <u>doesn't like</u> cats. Y like<u>s</u> cats.

   X and I <u>don't like</u> dogs. Y like<u>s</u> dogs.

2. Give each group the following instructions:

   > Tell the other people in your group how you feel about the items on the blackboard—whether you like them or not. Try to remember the opinions of the other people in your group about three of the items. You will report their opinions to another group. Remember to follow the model sentences on the blackboard.

3. Have the groups double up and report to their new, combined group about the likes and dislikes of their original group. Each person should try to report about at least one item.

Accountability: Ask the students to monitor and correct one another in the combined groups. You may want to have one or two groups write their collective opinions on the blackboard.

SUBJECT-VERB AGREEMENT

Theme: Working with plants and animals (Imagination)

Group Size: Three to five students

Goal: For each member of the group, agree on two or three daily tasks involving plants and animals.

1. Write on the blackboard:

   ZOO   CITY/STATE/NATIONAL PARK   FARM   RANCH

WASH	FEED	WATER	CLEAN	PLAY WITH
WALK	PLANT	SELL	CUT	BRUSH

   (Instead of writing the above words on the blackboard, you may prefer to brainstorm them with the class. Have the students think of places where people work with plants and animals, as well as verbs related to working with animals in such places.)

2. Give each group the following instructions:

   > Choose from the blackboard one of the places that have plants and animals. All of you are now working there. Discuss the kinds of jobs and responsibilities you have as employees, and decide on specific daily activities for each member of the group.

Accountability: Have a member of each group tell the class where the group works and what each person in the group does.

SUBJECT-VERB AGREEMENT

Theme: Household chores (Real information exchange)

Group Size: Three students

Goal: Decide which member of the group works the hardest in comparison with the rest of the group.

1. Write on the blackboard:

    My husband (wife) wash<u>es</u> the floors, do<u>es</u> the dishes, tak<u>es</u> out the garbage, and fix<u>es</u> everything that's broken. I do the laundry, prepare dinner, and break things for him (her) to fix.

2. Describe your own situation as a model, using the sentences you have written on the blackboard.

3. Give each group the following instructions:

    > Tell the other people in your group what the different members of your family or household do every day, every week, or every month as jobs or responsibilities at home. Also tell what your own duties are and whether it is a lot or a little work, compared to the other people in your household. (If you live alone, just tell the group what household jobs you do regularly.)

Accountability: Have a member of each group describe the work of its hardest-working member to the class. The class can decide who is the hardest-working person in the class. In humorous recognition of your hardest-working student's dubious new renown, you might want to ask him or her to erase the blackboard.

YES / NO QUESTIONS

Theme: Favorite foods, pastimes, and places to go (Real information exchange)

Group Size: Pairs

Goal: Guess what each partner is thinking, "Twenty Questions" style.

1. Write on the blackboard:

   FAVORITE FOOD

   FAVORITE PASTIME (FREE-TIME ACTIVITY)

   CITY TO VISIT

2. Tell the students the following:

   I am thinking of my favorite food. Try to guess what it is, using only questions that can be answered with *yes* or *no*. I will respond by nodding or shaking my head.

3. Let the students ask you questions until they guess the answer. Write model questions on the blackboard as they come, such as *Is it . . .?, Do you . . .?,* and so on.

4. Repeat steps 2 and 3, this time with your favorite pastime and the name of the city in the world you would most like to visit.

5. Ask the students to think of their own favorite food, their own favorite pastime, and a city in the world they would like very much to visit.

6. Give each pair the following instructions:

   > Ask your partner *yes/no* questions in order to guess his or her answers to the items on the blackboard. Your partner should only nod or shake his or her head—no speaking. Take turns guessing each other's answers. If you cannot guess an answer after five minutes, your partner may give you a little information to help you.
   >
   > Try to remember the last question you asked just before you guessed each answer.

Accountability: Ask eight to ten randomly selected students about the last question they asked before guessing their partner's answer. Have the class try to guess the answer based on that question. If this proves impossible, which it may, let the partner reveal the correct answer.

YES / NO QUESTIONS

Theme: The teacher (Real information exchange)

Group Size: Whole class

Goal: Guess information about the teacher by asking questions.

Materials: Small piece of chalk or other object concealable in one's fist

1. Write on the blackboard:

   1.   6.

   2.   7.

   3.   8.

   4.   9.

   5.   10.

2. Give the class the following instructions:

   > How well do you know me? Ask me *yes/no* questions about my likes and dislikes, about places I have visited, and so on, but don't make them too personal.
   >
   > If your question is correctly phrased, I will answer it secretly by putting this piece of chalk in my right hand for *yes*, and in my left hand for *no*. I will do this behind my back so that you cannot see. Before I show you my answer, I want you to try to guess what that answer is. One student will stand at the blackboard and count the number of students who think I said *yes* and the number who think I said *no*. After the count, I will show you which hand the chalk is in. If more than half the students are correct about my answer, I will give you a plus after the number of the question on the blackboard. If you are wrong, you will get a minus.
   >
   > I will answer ten questions, and at the end we can see how well you know me.

Accountability: Do not answer the questions unless they are perfectly correct. Let the students help one another if you prefer, or answer only questions that are perfectly correct to begin with, in order to make it more difficult.

Variation: Divide the class in two, possibly even separating males from females, to create a competition about who knows the teacher better. In this case, you would need two sets of numbers on the blackboard, and two students at the blackboard, one for each group.

INFORMATION QUESTIONS

Theme: Travel (Imagination)

Group Size: Pairs

Goal: Ask and answer questions about trips.

1. Put on the blackboard:

WHO?
WHERE?
WHEN?
WHY?
HOW LONG?
WHAT?

2. Give each pair the following instructions:

> One member of each pair should choose one of the means of transportation on the blackboard. Imagine that you have just taken a trip on this vehicle. Your partner will ask you questions about your trip. Use your imagination to answer the questions as you describe your trip. After you have been asked at least one question beginning with each of the question words on the blackboard, exchange roles and ask your partner about his or her trip on a different vehicle.
>
> Continue until you have discussed trips using all the pictures on the blackboard.

Accountability: Circulate during the exercise. Then, at the end, have several different students write on the blackboard the question they asked that received the most interesting, amusing, or unusual answer. After the questions are on the blackboard, have the writers' partners give the answers to the questions.

INFORMATION QUESTIONS

Theme: Your own school and general locale (Real information exchange)

Group Size: Pairs

Goal: Ask and answer questions about your school and town.

1. Write on the blackboard:

HOW MANY?	(name of your school)	(language of some students in your class)
WHERE?	(name of your city or town)	(location of some facilities in your school, such as the main office, library, etc.)
WHEN?	(starting time of your class)	
HOW LONG?	(length of your class)	(number of pages in your textbook)
WHO?	(location of some important building or monument in your town)	English
WHAT?	(name of your town's highest official)	(any other pertinent vital statistics about your students' environment)

    Sample blackboard (minus the question words):

Al-Khattabi High School		on the second floor	
Nador	8:00 a.m.	one hour	Room 408
every day	M–F	237	English
Berber	in the main building	in front of City Hall	Ahmed El-Oufi

2. Visibly count the number of students in the class, and write this number on the black-board. Tell the students that this is the answer to a question, and ask them to form the question. Write this model question on the blackboard:

    How many students are (there) in this class?

3. Give each pair the following instructions:

    > Take turns asking your partner the questions whose answers are on the black-board, just as we have done with the number of students in this class. All the words and expressions on the board are related to our class, school, or town. If your question is clear, your partner should be able to answer it using the ex-pressions on the blackboard. Continue asking and answering questions until you have used all of the words on the blackboard. You may continue with ques-tions of your own about our school or our town if you wish.

Accountability: When pairs have completed the activity, call on the students to give an appropriate question for each item on the blackboard.

QUESTIONS (ALL TYPES)

Theme: The teacher (Real information exchange)

Group Size: Whole class

Goal: Create a correct question for each piece of information on the blackboard.

1. Write on the blackboard:

At home.	After breakfast.	On weekends.
Yes, I do.	8:00.	Ten years.
No, I haven't.	Ten years ago.	. . .

(These should be short answers to questions about your life.)

2. Tell the class that the expressions on the blackboard are actually true answers to questions about your life. For some of the answers, there are many possible questions about your life that could all receive the same correct answer. For example, *Where do you prepare your lessons?* and *Where do you eat dinner?* could both be answered by *At home.*

3. Give the class the following instructions:

> Try to ask me questions about my life that would receive these answers on the blackboard. The question must be correctly phrased, or I will not answer it. If you ask me a correctly phrased question, but the answer is not on the blackboard, I will tell you that the answer is not on the blackboard.
>
> Each time someone asks me a correct question, and the answer to that question is on the blackboard, I will erase that answer. You must try to get all the answers on the blackboard erased.

Accountability: Answer only correctly phrased questions. Once the blackboard is erased, you may wish to continue the activity with individual students volunteering to come up front and write an answer of their own on the blackboard, which they will then answer for the class by responding to classmates' questions. Again, the volunteers should answer only correctly phrased questions.

Variation: Divide the class into two or more teams. Instead of erasing the answers, indicate which team phrased the question by putting a sign or number next to the answer. The team with its sign or number appearing on the blackboard the most times at the end of the activity wins.

QUESTIONS (ALL TYPES)

Theme: Ordinary possessions (Real information exchange)

Group Size: Pairs

Goal: Find people who own or possess eight objects before any other pair of students can do so.

Materials: Scrap paper

1. Write on the blackboard:

    something that someone might have with him or her right now

    something that someone might own . . . WHERE?

2. Give each pair the following instructions:

    > Think of four items that someone in the class might have with him or her right now, but which you yourselves (you and your partner) do not have with you today. Next, think of four items that someone in the class might own, but which neither you nor your partner owns.
    >
    > Write these items on two scraps of paper—each "paper" with two items that a person might have with him or her now, and two items that a person might own. For example (write on the blackboard):
    >
    > | PAPER 1 | PAPER 2 |
    > |---------|---------|
    > | eraser | stapler |
    > | mirror | scissors |
    > | CD player | motorcycle |
    > | basketball | telephone answering machine |
    >
    > When you and your partner have written down all eight items, each of you should take one of the two scraps of paper. Separate from your partner and walk around the room trying to find out who owns or has the items on your paper. If someone owns one of the items on your paper, find out where the item is. For example (write on the blackboard):
    > Do you have a _____ with you now?
    > Do you have a _____? Where is it?
    > Next to each item on your paper, write the name of a person who has it. Also write down where any "owned" item is. When you finish, come and tell me. The first pair with both partners done, wins.

Accountability: The winning pair receives as a prize any item on its list (pretend only), as long as the person who owns the item agrees to give it away. To verify accuracy during the activity, allow the students to ask you if you have the items on their lists. If the students are doing well, erase the model sentences on the blackboard.

QUESTIONS (ALL TYPES)

Theme: Games and sports (Real information exchange)

Group Size: Whole class (individuals circulating)

Goal: Form a team or find a partner for a specific sport or game.

Materials: Scrap paper

1. Write on the blackboard:

                    SPORT   GAME

    Do you play _____? How long have you played _____?

    Are you good at playing _____?

    (What position do you like to play?) When was the last time you played _____?

    How did you learn how to play _____? or Who taught you how to play _____?

2. Ask the students to each think of a game or a sport that they enjoy playing and that they play quite well. Tell them that they should try to think of a team activity, if possible, since they are going to try to put together a team for their game or sport. If students prefer games like tennis or chess, tell them to look for a good partner or opponent.

3. Give the class the following instructions:

> Walk around the classroom and ask every student if he or she plays your game or sport. If anyone says *yes*, ask questions like the ones on the blackboard to get more information about whether or not you might want that person on your team or as your partner. You are trying to find enough students to make a whole team, or the best possible partner.
>
> If you like another student's answers and think that student would be a good team member or partner, write down his or her name on a scrap of paper. When you have enough names to form a team or play a game, write the name of your sport or game with the names of all the players on the blackboard; then, return to the rest of your classmates to answer questions.

Accountability: Have the students come to the blackboard and answer a few questions about their teams or partners. The questions must come from the class. Note which names appear most frequently on the blackboard, in order to determine who are the real athletes, gamblers, and so on in the class.

To verify accuracy during the activity and to make it a little more interesting to the students, you (the teacher) could also participate.

SIMPLE PRESENT

Theme: Mystery movie (Imagination)

Group Size: Three students

Goal: Develop a mystery story which each member will retell to a new group.

Materials: Scrap paper for notes (optional)

1. Write on the blackboard:

   WHO   WHERE   HOW

        WHEN   WHY

2. Tell the students the following script for a mystery movie (or your own variation) two times. The first time, have them focus on the content; the second time, ask them to listen for tense.

   > My movie takes place during a very hot summer in a small town in central Florida. A young woman marries a very, very rich old man and moves into his big, old house. The year is 1965. The man is eighty years old when she marries him, so she thinks he won't live too much longer. But he does. He continues to live for another ten years. She, of course, is not getting any younger, so she starts to get impatient. She wants his money and his house as soon as possible. One evening at dinner, he tells her, "This soup tastes like poison!" He is right. He falls over dead on the floor. The woman finally is happy; she calls the bank and then the police. She thinks her problems are finished, but suddenly, a few days later, she gets a telephone call from the detective who will work on the case. His name is Lieutenant Columbo . . .

3. After your first telling of the mystery, have the students summarize the important parts of the plot. Refer to the words on the blackboard to help the students recall the story.

4. Now tell the story a second time and ask the students to listen for tense. After you've retold the story, ask:

   What tense did I use in that story? How did you know? Elicit the third-person singular-*s*.

5. Give each group the following instructions:

   > Using the simple present, create a group story for a mystery movie. Describe the events using the words on the blackboard. Each person in the group should be able to retell the whole story.

Accountability: Have the members of each group count off to three and form a <u>new</u> group of three with two other students who have the same number. If this process is too unwieldy, you can just tell the students to form new groups with two people who were not in their original group.

SIMPLE PRESENT (ACTION VERBS)

Theme: Daily habits and activities (Real information exchange)

Group Size: Five students

Goal: Find the two members of the group who have the most in common.

1. Draw on the blackboard.

2. Point to the clock picture on the blackboard and tell the students to ask you a question using *What time . . . ?* or *When . . . ?* Answer the question. Point to the kettle or one of the other pictures to elicit another question from the students. Answer the question and try to elicit still another question or two about the same picture, such as *What do you like to drink?* or *Do you like coffee or tea?* You will probably need to do a little coaching to get a variety of question types.

3. Point to one of the days of the week on the calendar picture and follow the same procedure as in step two. Again, try to elicit a variety of questions, such as *What do you do on Saturdays?* or *Where do you go on Saturday mornings?* Write a few sample questions and answers on the blackboard.

4. Give each group the following instructions:

> Ask and answer questions about your daily activities, referring to times and places (point to the calendar and the clock). Ask about jobs, eating and drinking habits, and so on. Refer to the blackboard for ideas. Remember to use the simple present tense because you are discussing repeated actions and habits. As you discuss one another's activities and habits, pay attention to which two people in your group seem to have the most similar daily lives.

Accountability: Have the two people with the most similar routines in each group stand up. Ask each partner to tell some of the things the other person does that are almost the same. Politely enforce the third-person singular suffix. Putting a giant *s* on the blackboard and pointing to it whenever students omit it can provide effective but gentle emphasis.

SIMPLE PRESENT (NON-ACTION VERBS)

Theme: Appearances (Imagination)

Group Size: Three students

Goal: Describe and guess pictures according to appearances.

1. Put on the blackboard:

look

seem

appear

have

She seems confused

He looks tired.

He has dimples.

2. Give each group the following instructions:

> Make sure that all members of your group can see the blackboard easily and clearly. One person will start. That person should choose one of the faces on the blackboard and describe it, using one of the verbs on the blackboard in the simple present tense, as in the model sentences. The other two people in the group should try to guess which picture is being described. Whoever guesses the correct picture first goes next. He or she should then choose a new picture and describe it for the group to guess. Use each picture more than once; continue until you have described every picture at least two times.
>
> For example, if I say *She has long hair,* which picture am I describing? (Let a student guess, and have that student do the next one as further modeling.)

Accountability: Have volunteers describe the pictures. Encourage the students to say more than one thing about each picture, such as *She looks very sad and she has long hair.* After each picture has been described, erase it. Continue until the blackboard is empty.

SIMPLE PRESENT (NON-ACTION VERBS)

Theme: Personal information (Real information exchange)

Group Size: Pairs, then groups of two pairs each

Goal: Tell a new pair of classmates about one's original partner.

Materials: Scrap paper for notes

1. Write on the blackboard:

food	sports		like	love	hate
music	weekends		believe in		think (opinion)
people	education		know	feel	
places	health		own	understand	
work	weather				

I don't like hot weather.   I love chocolate.   I hate spiders.

I believe in hard work.   I don't own a bicycle.

2. Give each pair the following instructions:

> Use the verbs listed on the blackboard to discuss with your partner the topics that are also listed on the blackboard. You may ask and answer questions, or you can just tell each other about yourselves. Take notes, because you will be using the information about your partner later.

3. After the students have had time to get eight to ten pieces of information about their partners, combine each pair with another pair to form a new group of four students.

4. Give each new group the following instructions:

> Tell the people in your new group about your original partner, using as many of the verbs on the blackboard as you can. Be sure to use the appropriate third-person singular form, and correct one another whenever necessary.

Accountability: For each of the eight to ten categories on the left side of the blackboard, ask for one or two volunteers to tell something about a person in their group.

PRESENT CONTINUOUS

Theme: Activities associated with various places (Pantomime)

Group Size: Pairs

Goal: Communicate an activity through pantomime.

1. Write on the blackboard:

kitchen	living room	restaurant
bathroom	beach	store or market
library	garden	park
stadium	zoo	theater

2. Give each pair the following instructions:

> Look at the places I have written on the blackboard. Think about activities that people do in each of these places. They must be activities that you can demonstrate. One at a time, I am going to call out the name of one of these places to you. Immediately try to think of an activity that people do in this place and that you can pantomime (demonstrate or show without talking, just using your hands and body) for your partner to guess. As soon as your partner thinks he or she knows what you are doing, he or she should tell you. If your partner is correct, raise your hand. Partners who are guessing, be sure to use the present continuous tense.
>
> When all (or most) of you have raised your hands, we'll try a new place from the list on the blackboard.

3. Tell the students that before you begin, you are going to do one practice round. Select a strong student to be your partner, preferably bringing him or her to the front of the room. Write the word *classroom* on the blackboard, and then call it out. If the student partner does not do anything right away, indicate that you have an idea yourself, and start pantomiming writing on the blackboard. Your student should be able to guess what you are doing. If the student comes up with an idea first, say what he or she is doing. Write the model answer on the blackboard, such as *The teacher is writing on the blackboard*, or *You are writing on the blackboard.*

Accountability: At the end of each round (that is, when most or all pairs have indicated that they are finished by one partner's having raised a hand), have one pair stand. While one partner pantomimes, the other partner will tell what he or she is doing.

PRESENT CONTINUOUS

Theme: Household activities (Imagination)

Group Size: Five or more students

Goal: Try to remember some of the more interesting or amusing suggestions from the group.

1. Put on the blackboard

2. Give each group the following instructions:

> Look through this window. Inside, you will see five people—an old man, a baby, two young women, a teenage boy—and a kitten. What are these people doing? Use your imagination and tell the other members of your group what you see. Tell what the kitten is doing as well as what each person is doing as you are looking through the window. Use the present continuous tense to describe what is happening now. Before you begin, you may want to decide which room or rooms you are looking into. Everyone should participate. Your group may even want to make up a little story.

3. Tell the students that before they begin, you want to tell them what you see. Look through the window and tell them what room you are looking into and what each person is doing. You may want to write a few examples on the blackboard.

Accountability: Roll up a piece of paper to look like a telescope. The "telescope" emphasizes the immediacy of the event. You may not want to do this with your class if it might appear impolite to some students. Hand it to the students as you have them look through the window and tell the class some of the things that the people inside are doing, according to their groups. Have one member of each group do this.

PRESENT CONTINUOUS

Theme: Billboard advertising (Imagination)

Group Size: Three to five students

Goal: Agree on a product to be advertised and design an ad for it.

1. Draw on the blackboard:

2. Give each group the following instructions:

> Design an advertisement for this billboard. First, decide what product your group would like to advertise. It could be the object in the woman's hand, but it does not have to be. Next, plan a dialogue, or conversation, for your ad. What is she saying? What is he saying? What are they doing? Do not actually name the product in your ad, however. You are going to present your ad to the other groups, and they will try to guess the product you are advertising.

3. Tell the students that before they begin, you will give them a sample ad to guess about. Point to the billboard drawing on the blackboard as you present the following:

    The man is saying, "Is that new?"

    The woman is smiling at the small black object in her hands and saying, "No. I bought it ten years ago, and it still sounds as good as it did the day I bought it."

    What is this an ad for?

    Answer: A portable radio

Accountability: Have one or more members of each group come to the blackboard and present their advertisement to the class for guessing. Be sure to enforce their use of the present continuous tense as they describe their ad.

Variation: As the class guesses the product, instead of having the students call it out, have anyone who thinks he or she knows the answer come to the blackboard and draw the product in the woman's hands. If you choose to do the activity this way, include the drawing task in the practice example about the radio.

PRESENT CONTINUOUS

Theme: Household activities (Imagination)

Group Size: Whole class

Goal: Tell what various people in one's household are doing right now, in an ideal world.

1. Put on the blackboard:

2. Give the class the following instructions:

> The person or people you live with (indicate people on the blackboard) have just come out of a "perfection machine" that has made them into <u>perfect</u> people. What are the perfect people in your house doing right now? Use the present continuous tense, such as, *My husband is washing <u>my</u> car.*

Accountability: As a whole-class activity, accountability is built in. As the students volunteer their answers, write some on the blackboard. After enough people have responded correctly in the present continuous tense, erase those models.

Variation: This activity can also be done using a picture of a window, which you can draw very simply on the blackboard (use the model on page 23). Have the students look through the window to see what the people they live with are doing.

                     This activity can also be used to talk about people outside the household, such as family and/or friends in general. You can give examples, such as *My mother is sending me a thousand dollars.* or *My sister is writing me a long letter.*

PRESENT CONTINUOUS VS. SIMPLE PRESENT

Theme: Change in routine, travel (Imagination)

Group Size: Pairs

Goal: Create a sentence or sentences about an imaginary person, whose nationality the class will guess.

1. Put on the blackboard:

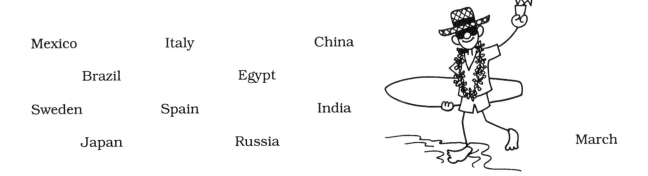

Mexico   Italy   China

    Brazil   Egypt

Sweden   Spain   India

    Japan   Russia   March

He <u>usually dances</u> the flamenco, but <u>this week</u> he <u>is dancing</u> the hula.

He <u>usually wears</u> boots, but <u>this week</u> he <u>is wearing</u> nothing on his feet.

2. Tell the class the following story:

> This tourist is visiting Hawaii this week. It is March. (Indicate the blackboard.) He comes from one of the countries on the blackboard, and you are going to decide which country he is from. He loves Hawaii. Everything he is doing there this week is different from what he usually does in his country.
>
> I am going to tell you what he usually does, which is different from what he is doing this week. Try to guess the country he is from. For example, if I say, *He usually dances the flamenco, but this week he is dancing the hula*, what country do you think he is from? (Answer: Spain.) If I tell you, *He usually wears boots, but this week he is wearing nothing on his feet*, what country might he be from? (Possible answers: Sweden, Russia, Japan, China, and so on.)

3. Give each pair the following instructions:

> Choose a country that you would like this tourist to be from. Create a sentence or sentences describing what he usually does that is different from what he is doing this week in Hawaii. Create enough sentences for the class to be able to guess exactly which country your tourist is from.

Accountability: Have each pair write its sentence(s) on the blackboard for the class to guess.

SIMPLE PAST

Theme: Today's activities (Real information exchange)

Group Size: Three students

Goal: Reconstruct one another's day using the simple past tense.

1. Put on the blackboard:

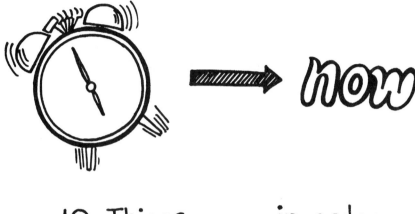

10 Things —— in order

2. Tell the students to listen very carefully and try to remember as much as they can of what you are about to say. Then, tell them about ten different things that you did today before class, in order, beginning with when you got up.

3. Have two student volunteers try to retell the story of your day, alternating and helping each other as they go.

4. Give each group the following instructions:

> One at a time, tell one another what you did today from the time you got up until now. Use the simple past tense to describe your days. Do not exceed ten things, if possible.
>
> Immediately after each person finishes, the other two members of your group should try to retell the events, alternating and helping each other when necessary.

Accountability: The students should monitor and correct one another during the retelling portion of the activity. You might also circulate to help with irregular past tense forms. Any group that finishes early can write the day's events of one of its group members on the blackboard.

SIMPLE PAST

Theme: Original story (Imagination)

Group Size: Three students

Goal: Create an original story using six objects, and be prepared to retell the story.

Materials: Objects produced by students on the spot

1. Write on the blackboard:

> 6 OBJECTS, including   money
>
> a document
>
> 4 other objects—any kind

"Once upon a time . . ."

2. Give each group the following instructions:

> Tell a story in the past tense using six objects that you have with you. Look in your pockets, purses, and bags to find objects that could help you tell this story. One of your objects should be money, and one of them should be a document of some kind, such as a driver's license or an identification card. The more unusual the objects, the better.
>
> Start with the expression *Once upon a time . . .*, and choose one of the objects to begin. Continue your story using each of the other five objects, one at a time. Physically place the objects next to one another, in order, as your story develops.
>
> Be sure to tell your story in the simple past tense. In fact, tell us exactly when it happened—at some specific time in the past.

3. As each group finishes its story, have one member of the group come up to the blackboard and write the verbs only, in past tense, from their story.

4. When all the groups have completed their verb lists, review each list and make any necessary corrections.

Accountability: One at a time, have each group come up to the front of the class with its objects and tell its story to the rest of the class. The verb list and the objects will help jog the group's memories. Encourage more than one member of each group to do the talking, which should be a mutually supportive group effort.

SIMPLE PAST

Theme: Family (Imagination)

Group Size: Three to five students

Goal: Create a group story and be prepared to both tell it and write it.

1. Draw on the blackboard:

2. Give each group the following instructions:

> Using the six pictures on the blackboard <u>in any order</u>, make up a story that
> includes every picture. You need only one sentence for each picture. Use the
> simple past tense.

Accountability: Have a student from each group write the story on the blackboard. When all
the stories have been written on the blackboard, have one other student
from each group read its story to the class. During the reading, ask a student from a different group to stand at the blackboard and try to point to the
appropriate picture as the story is being read.

USED TO (PAST)

Theme: Retired people and past professional lives (Role play)

Group Size: Three students

Goal: Decide which person in the group had the best life or job, and which person had the most difficult one.

1. Put on the blackboard:

USED TO + simple form
  patients
  students
  clients

2. Tell the students that the three older people on the blackboard are all retired professionals. One of them used to be a doctor, one of them used to be a lawyer, and one of them used to be a university professor.

3. Tell the students that they are going to be discussing some of the things these people used to do when they were still working—things they used to <u>have</u> to do and things they used to <u>like</u> to do. Brainstorm and write on the blackboard some of the things that these people might have done when they were working in their professions. Describe their duties, phone calls, schedules, pressures, free time, vacations, and so on.

4. Give each group the following instructions:

> Each of you will pretend to be one of the three older people in the picture. Talk about the things you <u>used to</u> do when you were still working. Be sure to mention the good things and the bad things.
>
> After you have discussed your professional lives for several minutes, start talking about which one of you had the best life or job and which one had the most difficult situation.

Accountability: First, get a class count by a show of hands to see which retired person had the best life or job, and which the most difficult one. Put the class statistics on the blackboard. Then, ask a member of each group to report its decision about the best and/or the most difficult job, and to give one dramatic example to illustrate what that retired person used to do.

USED TO VS. SIMPLE PAST

Theme: Neighbors (Imagination)

Group Size: Three to five students

Goal: Create a group story and be prepared to share it with the class.

1. Draw on the blackboard:

2. Tell the students about the noisy dog that used to live next door to you. As you tell the story, write the sentences on the blackboard:

    A dog <u>used to live</u> next door to me.

    He <u>used to bark</u> all night.

    Sometimes he even <u>used to howl</u>. (Imitate the sound.)

    Finally, I <u>asked</u> my neighbor to do something. He <u>did</u>. He <u>moved</u> away.

3. Give each group the following instructions:

    > You all used to live together in the same house. Just like me, you had a problem with your neighbors. What are some of the things that they used to do that bothered you? In your group, discuss at least five different things that your neighbors <u>used to</u> do that made you angry and upset.
    >
    > What did you finally do to end your problems? Decide what actions you took that made your neighbors stop doing what they were doing. Be creative, imaginative, and dramatic. Remember to use the simple past tense when you describe what you did to stop your neighbors. Be ready to tell the class your ideas.

Accountability: Have one member of each group tell the class at least two of the things that the neighbors did; have another member tell what the group did to stop them. Correct any sentences with errors by writing them on the blackboard to keep everyone's interest, and to focus on form.

USED TO VS. SIMPLE PAST

Theme: Tricks (Real information exchange)

Group Size: Five students

Goal: Select the best trick to share with the class.

1. Write on the blackboard:

	parents
TRICKS	teachers
	brothers/sisters
	friends
	pets

2. Tell the students about a trick that you <u>used to</u> play on people when you were young. Be sure to make it clear that it was something you did again and again. Write the trick on the blackboard, such as:

   When I was a child, my father <u>used to come</u> into my bedroom every night to kiss me goodnight. Sometimes, I <u>used to pretend</u> to be asleep.

3. Tell the students about a trick that you <u>once</u> played on someone, beginning your sentence with *One time . . .* Write it on the blackboard, such as:

   One time I <u>got</u> in bed with my feet at the top of the bed, instead of my head, and my father <u>came</u> in and <u>kissed</u> my feet.

4. Give each group the following instructions:

   > Tell one another some of the tricks you used to play when you were a young child. Use *used to* if you did it many times; use the simple past tense if you did it only one time. (You may want to review the verbs in the sentences on the blackboard at this point.) Plan to tell the rest of the class about any really good tricks from your group.

Accountability: Have one student from each group tell the best trick, in his or her opinion, that he or she heard from another student in the group.

Variation: If you have a very advanced class that is ready to practice the distinction between *used to* and *would* (after the past tense already has been established), add it to your example . . . *when my father would come into my bedroom* . . . Hold the students responsible for the *would* form in the reporting phase.

PAST CONTINUOUS

Theme: Past activities (Real information exchange)

Group Size: Whole class (individuals circulating)

Goal: Try to find another student who was doing the same thing at the same time in the past.

1. Write on the blackboard:

    SEASON   YEAR IN THE PAST (not more than 15 years ago)

2. Tell the students to think of a season (summer, fall, winter, spring) and a year in the past, but not more than 15 years ago. (This limit will vary according to the age of your students. Do not pre-date anyone's birth.) Write examples on the board:

                summer, 1985   fall, 1992

3. Give the class the following instructions:

    > Walk around the class asking other students what they were doing during the season and year that you have chosen. Ask and answer questions using the past continuous tense. Try to find another student who was doing the same thing you were during your chosen year and season.

4. Tell the students that before you begin, you will do a few practice examples with the whole class. Point to your first example and ask a student, *What were you doing in summer, 1985?* Let the student answer; then erase *summer, 1985.* Repeat the question and answer with *fall, 1992;* then erase the cue. (The reason for erasing the cues is that sometimes the students think they are supposed to use those examples rather than their own. The result can be a whole class asking one another the same question.) Complete the practice example with two volunteer students—one asking a question about the season and year that he or she chose, and the other answering it.

Accountability: Have the students who found someone who was doing the same thing write about their experience(s) on the blackboard. They should write in past continuous tense, such as *Ali and I were traveling in summer, 1993.*

PAST CONTINUOUS

Theme: Activities on a train (Imagination)

Group Size: Three or four students (as many groups as there are train cars on the blackboard)

Goal: Prepare five sentences to present to the class.

Materials: Scrap paper for notes (optional)

1. Draw on the blackboard:

2. Tell the students that this train had to make a sudden stop because too much noise, wild movement, and other things were happening on the train. For example, (write on the blackboard):

   An old woman <u>was hitting</u> people on the head with her purse.

3. (Assign each train car to a different group of students.) Give each group the following instructions:

   > Decide together what was happening in your group's car that forced the conductor to stop the train. Discuss at least five different people or events in your car and be ready to share them with the class. Remember to use the past continuous tense because these events were still happening when the train was stopped.

Accountability: Have one or two members of each group report to the class about what was happening in their car.

PAST CONTINUOUS VS. SIMPLE PAST

Theme: Burglary (Imagination)

Group Size: Three to five students

Goal: Prepare five sentences, one about each room.

Materials: Scrap paper for notes (optional)

1. Put on the blackboard:

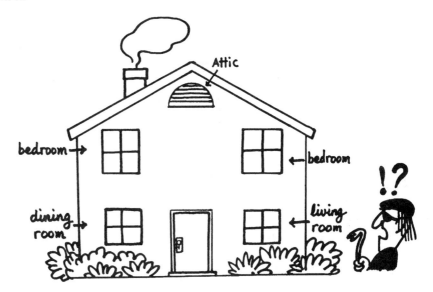

2. Tell the students the following story:

    One night a burglar came to this house to rob it. But before he went in, he decided to look into every room to see if anybody was home and to find out what the people were doing. He looked into each room, and he was surprised. There was one person in every room, and each person was doing something very strange when the burglar looked in. He saw such strange things that he decided not to go into that house, and he left. For example (write this sentence on the blackboard):

    When he looked in the living room, a woman <u>was playing</u> the piano with her feet.

3. Give each group the following instructions:

    > Decide who was in each room and what that person was doing when the burglar looked inside. Write or prepare to say a complete sentence about each of the five rooms.

Accountability: Have a member of each group present what they saw to the class.

PAST CONTINUOUS VS. SIMPLE PAST

Theme: Rescue (Imagination)

Group Size: Three to five students

Goal: Agree on a situation to describe and draw for the class.

1. Put on the blackboard:

WAS/WERE
_____ing

SAVED/HELPED/
FOUND

2. Tell the students to look at the picture on the blackboard and decide whether it shows a good situation or a dangerous one. Then ask them to suggest someone or something that could save these people from going over the waterfall. Use their suggestions to describe the whole scene, using the past continuous tense, and the rescue, using the simple past tense. To help establish past time, you might give the event a date or some other identifying point in the past, such as *last summer.* If no student comes up with a suggestion, you could have a giant tree fall across the top of the waterfall, have the water cut off from a dam upstream, or have a strong wind or tornado whisk the people to safety.

3. Give each group the following instructions:

> Think of a dangerous situation involving three to five people. Tell what each person <u>was doing</u> when someone or something <u>saved, helped,</u> or <u>found</u> them. Remember to use the past continuous tense when you describe what the people were already doing, and the simple past tense when you describe the rescue. (Review the picture on the blackboard one more time, pointing at the people; for example, say, *A man was swimming.* Repeat the rescue in the simple past tense.)

Accountability: Have a student from each group tell its story to the class while another student from that group draws the situation on the blackboard. (Larger groups make it easier to find an artist in each one.)

Variation: If a dangerous situation is inappropriate for your students, have them think of an entertaining outdoor event interrupted by rain. You could adapt the waterfall scene on the blackboard to look like a lake and introduce a thunderstorm.

SIMPLE FUTURE

Theme: Class party (Imagination)

Group Size: Three to five students (of similar age and/or interests, if possible)

Goal: Plan a party and be prepared to describe the plan to the class.

Materials: Scrap paper for notes (optional)

1. Write on the blackboard:

A PARTY   time and place—when, where

food and drink—what, who

decorations—what, where, who

music—what, who, equipment

furniture arrangement—what, where

activities—games, dancing, professional entertainment

cost—how much, who pays?

2. Give each group the following instructions:

> Plan a party for the class. When and where will the party take place? What kind
> of food and drinks will there be? Who will bring what? As you discuss your plan,
> use all the suggestions on the blackboard. Be extravagant, wild, and creative.
> Use the simple future tense.

Accountability: One at a time, have a student from each group come to the front of the class
to describe the party. This follow-up may best be done as a question-and-
answer session to include the practice of simple future questions and to
insure class attention. As each group reports its information, you should
take notes on the blackboard, labeling the groups in some fashion (with
numbers or names, for example) above each group's list of party data. When
every group has reported, take a class vote on the best possible party idea.
Tell the students <u>not</u> to vote for their own group.

Variation: Plan and have a real party using all or part of the group plans.

SIMPLE FUTURE

Theme: Future events (Imagination)

Group Size: Four or five students

Goal: Agree on six events or conditions, three good and three bad, that will happen in the future.

1. Write on the blackboard:

   3 GOOD THINGS

                              NEXT 100 YEARS

   3 BAD THINGS

2. Give each group the following instructions:

   > Discuss and reach agreement on three good things and three bad things that you think will probably happen in the next 100 years. The good things and the bad things that you agree on must be consistent with one another. In other words, they <u>all</u> must be possible—one example cannot prevent any of the others from happening. Remember to use the simple future tense.

Accountability: Have volunteer members of each group tell the class what their group decided. As the students report, write the results on the blackboard and find out by a show of hands how many other groups had the same ideas. In order to avoid redundancy and speed up the information-sharing part of this activity, ask the students to report only new ideas.

SIMPLE FUTURE

Theme: Travel (Imagination)

Group Size: Three students

Goal: Develop a travel plan, which each group member will tell to a new group.

Materials: Scrap paper for notes (optional)

1. Put on the blackboard:

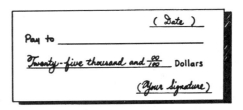

HAWAII   PARIS   TIBET   GREECE   JAPAN

what to take   how long to stay   transportation   sightseeing trips

food   hotel   shopping   entertainment

2. Ask each student in the class to choose one of the destinations on the blackboard and write it down. Then, tell the students to each form a group with two other students who chose the same place.

3. Announce to the students that each group will receive a check for $25,000 (indicate the check on the blackboard) for a trip to their chosen destination.

4. Tell the students that you also will receive a check for you and two other teachers, and that the three of you are taking a trip to Rome. Write your plans on the blackboard:

   <u>We'll stay</u> for three weeks.

   <u>We'll fly</u> first class.

   <u>We'll</u> each <u>buy</u> five pairs of Italian shoes.

5. Give each group the following instructions:

   > Plan together how you will spend the money for this trip. Discuss the items suggested on the blackboard. If necessary, take notes to remember details. Use the simple future tense.

Accountability: Have the students form new groups of three or more, but with students who made plans for a different destination. Each student will tell the new group about the original group's plans. Each new group should decide on the best trip from the ones presented.

FUTURE CONTINUOUS

Theme: Future activities (Real information exchange)

Group Size: Whole class (individuals circulating)

Goal: Ask and answer questions in the future continuous tense, according to a partner's cues.

Materials: Scrap paper and a straight pin for each student

1. Put on the blackboard:

2. Divide the class in half. Have one half of the class choose a time (indicating a.m. or p.m.) of day or night. Tell the students to write the time in large numbers on a small scrap of paper and pin it to their shirts. Have the other half of the class choose a day of the week, or just *tomorrow*, and write it on a scrap of paper, which they, too, will pin to their shirts.

3. Pin a tag on yourself that says *9:30 p.m.* Find a student who has a day of the week written on his or her tag, and ask the question, *What will you be doing (Wednesday) at 9:30 p.m.?* Write the question on the blackboard, using the day on the student's tag. Write the student's answer on the blackboard, also in the future continuous tense. Then, have the first student find another student, this time someone with a time written on his or her tag. Repeat the example with these two students.

4. Give the class the following instructions:

> Move around the class from student to student, asking and answering questions about the next seven days using the future continuous tense. You must always find a partner with a different type of tag than you have. For example, if you have a day on your tag, you must find a person who has a time. If you have a time on your tag, find someone with a day. This way, you can make complete questions and answers. If your tag says *7:30 a.m.* and your partner's tag says *Sunday*, then you will ask each other, *What will you be doing Sunday at 7:30 a.m.?*

Accountability: Ask those students who found someone with the same plans for the same time to write complete sentences about their activities on the blackboard such as, *Ching and I will be walking in the park Sunday at 3:00 p.m.*

FUTURE CONTINUOUS

Theme: Schedules, future activities (Imagination)

Group Size: Pairs

Goal: Ask and answer questions about a schedule, using the future continuous tense.

1. Put on the blackboard:

	SU	M	TU	W	TH	F	SA
MORN	Sleep late	Relax	Work	Drive back from Las Vegas	Dentist	Work	Work
AFT	Play Basketball	Work	Drive to Las Vegas	Rest	Work	Work	Shop
EVE	Movie	Watch TV	Gamble	Dinner at Mom's	Watch TV	Baseball Game	Dance

2. Have the students look at the schedule on the blackboard. Explain that it is Mike Miller's schedule for next week. He works as an auto mechanic and lives in Los Angeles. Tell the students that they will be asking and answering questions about Mike's schedule, working in pairs, but only one partner will be looking at the blackboard. The other partner will be facing away from the blackboard. The partner who is not looking at the blackboard will ask questions; the partner who is looking at the blackboard will answer.

3. Before having half the class turn away from the blackboard, give each pair the following instructions:

> The partner who cannot see the blackboard should ask questions about a specific day and time of day next week, such as *2:00 Monday afternoon, 8:00 Tuesday evening,* and so on. Ask only one question about each day—one for Monday, one for Tuesday, . . . Use the future continuous tense. For example (write on the blackboard), *What will Mike be doing next Wednesday morning at 10:00?* The other partner will answer, *He'll be driving back from Las Vegas.*
>
> After one of you has asked seven questions (about seven days), exchange places with your partner and reverse roles. The new partner who cannot see the blackboard should use different days and times from the ones the first partner did.

4. Have one partner in each pair face away from the blackboard. It is helpful if you demonstrate and emphasize a very specific chair arrangement with a sample pair in front of the class.

Accountability: Erase the blackboard and ask questions about Mike. Have the students volunteer answers based on memory; there should almost always be someone who remembers the answer from the blackboard.

FUTURE CONTINUOUS

Theme: Travel (Imagination)

Group Size: Pairs

Goal: Answer a partner's questions about a trip, making it sound as attractive as possible so that the partner can decide whether or not to come along.

1. Write on the blackboard:

                                        will be doing

do   Where?

visit   When?

spend   How long?

go   How much?

take   What?

return   How (Transportation)?

stay

2. Give each pair the following instructions:

> One of you will be Partner A and one of you will be Partner B. Partner A, think of a place to which you would like to travel. Answer the questions that Partner B asks you about this trip. Use the future continuous tense in your answers, because you are talking about future plans. (Remember, *I will be visiting the Great Wall of China* means that you are <u>planning</u> to do that.) Try to make your trip sound like a wonderful one. Don't worry about money. You want Partner B to agree to come along.
>
> Partner B, ask questions to help you decide whether or not you want to go along on Partner A's trip. Use the words on the blackboard in your questions. Be prepared to tell the class why you are going or not going.
>
> After Partner B has asked and Partner A has answered questions about all the items on the blackboard, and after Partner B has decided whether to go along on the trip, reverse roles.

Accountability: Have Partner B tell the class whether or not he or she wants to go along on the trip and why, using the future continuous tense.

PRESENT PERFECT

Theme: City parks (Imagination)

Group Size: Whole class (divided in half)

Goal: Create a half-finished city park

1. Draw on the blackboard two very large rectangles, as far away from each other as possible:

2. Brainstorm with the class what city parks usually have—ponds, fountains, museums, cafes, tennis courts, gardens, playgrounds, and so on—and write the results on the blackboard in a column with space to the right. Next to each item, add the appropriate verb of construction. For example:

   trees—plant
   playground—build/construct/put in
   pond—dig/fill
   statue—put up/erect
   (a minimum of ten such items)

   Also write these sample sentences on the blackboard:

   Trees <u>have been planted</u> already. The playground <u>has not been built</u> yet.

3. Divide the class into two separate groups, arranging each group as close to one of the rectangles as possible in order to minimize distractions.

4. Give each group the following instructions:

   > Create a city park that is only half finished. Work as a group to decide what has been done already, and what has not been done yet. Use the examples on the blackboard. Choose half of the ideas on the blackboard to have been done already, and the other half to have not been done yet. Have someone in your group draw in the rectangle each idea for something that has been completed. For the things you decide have not been done, make a note on the blackboard next to your group's rectangle.

Accountability: Ask a member of each group to describe what has and has not been done.

Variation: If your class is not very familiar with city parks, you might have the groups describe the completion of a building such as a school or private house.

43

PRESENT PERFECT

Theme: Unusual experiences (Real information exchange)

Group Size: Four or five students

Goal: Each group member should come up with something that only he or she has done.

1. Write on the blackboard a question based on your own unusual experience, such as

   Has anyone ever walked through a two-mile underground tunnel?

   Has anyone ever + (past participle) . . .?

2. Ask the class the question that you have written on the blackboard. It should be something that you have done, but that you are reasonably sure no one else in the class has done. When no one responds affirmatively (you may need a few additional possibilities for back-up), say, *I have.*

3. Give each group the following instructions:

   > Take two or three minutes to try to think of some things that you have done, but that you think no one else in your group has ever done. After everyone in your group has thought of one or two things, take turns asking the other members of your group if any of them has ever done it.
   >   If someone in your group says he or she has already done it, then try to think of another example. Each of you should try to find something that only <u>you</u> have done.

Accountability: Have a member of each group share one or two of the more interesting examples of something that only one person in the group has done.

PRESENT PERFECT (VS. SIMPLE PAST— OPTIONAL)

Theme: Unusual animals (Real information exchange)

Group Size: Whole class (individuals circulating)

Goal: Mentally note any interesting answers.

Materials: Scrap paper and a straight pin for each student

1. Write on the blackboard:

   unusual animal: (including insects,   SEE—1
                        reptiles, birds, etc.)   EAT—2

                                                   RIDE—3

2. Have each student think of an unusual (if possible) animal—not a dog or cat.

3. Have students count off to three. The students who are number one should write *see* on a scrap of paper and pin it to the front of their shirts. Number twos should make and wear tags with *eat*, and number threes should do the same with *ride.*

4. Give the students the following instructions:

   > Walk around the room and ask as many of your classmates as possible if they have ever seen, eaten, or ridden (according to the word pinned to your shirt) the animal you chose. Use the present perfect tense for your question.

   (Optional: If someone answers *yes*, ask that person when and where he or she saw, ate, or rode it. Ask and answer these questions in the simple past tense, since it probably happened only once, at a very specific time in the past.)

5. Before beginning the activity, ask a few students sample questions about an animal of your own. Write the question on the blackboard with the students' answers, such as:

   Have you ever _____ a skunk?

   Yes, I have. No, I haven't.

   (Optional: When and where did you _____ it? I _____ it . . .)

Accountability: Ask the students to volunteer any unusual, unexpected, or interesting answers they received. They should describe these answers directly and avoid reported speech. You might write a model sentence on the blackboard, such as *Ingrid has eaten a snake.*

PRESENT PERFECT VS. PRESENT PERFECT CONTINUOUS

Theme: New and old habits (Real information exchange)

Group Size: Pairs

Goal: Make a mental note of a partner's more interesting answers, in order to ask for further information about them.

1. Write on the blackboard:

RECENTLY		do	watch	go
		eat	shop	get up

2. Have the students ask you some questions about your recent activities and habits on weekends. When you get questions requiring the present perfect continuous tense, write them on the blackboard. Tell the students to ask about a particular day and time of day, such as Friday evening:

   What <u>have you been eating</u> for breakfast on Sunday mornings recently?

   Answer the questions in the present perfect continuous tense.

3. Give each pair the following instructions:

   > Discuss the past three or four weekends with your partner. Ask and answer questions using the present perfect continuous tense because you are interested only in recent activities and habits. You may need to ask a more general question first, in some cases (such as *Do you shop on weekends?* and *When exactly do you shop? Saturday mornings? Sunday afternoons?*), before asking, *Where have you been shopping on Saturday mornings?*
   >
   > Try to ask questions using all the "wh" words: *where, what, when, who,* and *how.* Pay attention to and remember any interesting activities and habits of your partner.

4. After most pairs have had time to ask and answer at least five questions each, give them the following further instructions (to be modeled by you in step 5):

> Now ask your partner new questions about some of the activities you remember. You want to find out if these are new habits or old ones. Because we generally use the non-continuous present perfect tense for questions about a person's whole life (unless the whole life is referred to explicitly, as in *Have you been doing that all your life?*), use the following model to ask the questions (write on the blackboard):
>
> Have you always _____ on Saturday mornings?
>
> Reply to your partner's questions using the present perfect tense with *always* (if it is an old habit), or the present perfect continuous tense with *recently* or *only recently* (if it is a new one).

5. Before letting students begin step 4, have them practice by asking you the same further information about your habits as you described them in step 2. Write a sample exchange on the blackboard, such as:

    <u>Have you always eaten</u> cereal for breakfast on Sunday mornings?

    No, <u>I have only recently been eating</u> cereal.

    Yes, <u>I have always eaten cereal</u> on Sunday mornings.

Accountability: Try to get responses from as many students as possible by saying, *Tell me about your partner.* Guide the students into using the correct tense. If you put a model on the blackboard, erase it after three or four students have reported. Here is a sample response format:

My partner has been _____ing recently, but she (he) has always _____.

PAST PERFECT

Theme: Arriving late (Real information exchange)

Group Size: Three students

Goal: Choose the most interesting story to tell the class.

1. Put on the blackboard:

When Tim got to the party, they <u>had already finished</u> the cake.

"   "   they ha<u>d already opened</u> the presents.

2. Tell the students the following story about the pictures on the blackboard:

> This is Tim. He was invited to a birthday party yesterday, but he got there very late—two hours late! Many things had already happened by the time he got there. For example, they had already finished the cake and opened the presents. (Indicate the model sentences on the blackboard.)

3. Brainstorm with the students a few more things that Tim might have missed and write them on the blackboard.

4. Give each group the following instructions:

> Think of a time (or several times) when you were too late for something, and when you got there, some important things had already happened. It might have been a meeting, a class, a bus or a train, a job interview or a job, an appointment, a theater or sports event, or something else that you remember. Be sure to use the past perfect tense for the things that had already happened when you arrived. Listen for interesting stories or situations to share with the class.

Accountability: Have a member of each group tell the most interesting story, preferably not his or her own.

Variation: If students seem unable to think of real examples, you could have the groups create an amusing or exciting situation from their imaginations.

PAST PERFECT

Theme: Puppies (Imagination)

Group Size: Four to five students

Goal: After thinking up four or five ideas, write them on the blackboard.

1. Put on the blackboard:

knock over
wet
tear
chew up
destroy

2. Tell the class the following story:

   Pat and Pete went out to dinner one evening and they forgot to put their new puppy outside. Of course, while they were gone, the puppy did some terrible things inside the house. What did it do?

3. Write the following example on the blackboard:

   By the time Pat and Pete got back, the puppy <u>had knocked over</u> a lamp, <u>had eaten</u> the cat's food, and <u>had pulled</u> the TV on the floor.

4. Give each group the following instructions:

   > Discuss some of the awful things that the puppy had done by the time Pat and Pete got back at 11:00.

5. Before having the groups begin, review the vocabulary on the blackboard. They will need it.

Accountability: Have a student from each group write some of the group's ideas on the blackboard. If your class is large, begin this process while the groups are still discussing the puppy story. Correct the sentences together on the blackboard.

PAST PERFECT

Theme: Hearsay (Real information exchange)

Group Size: Three students

Goal: Find one item that everyone in a group had heard and that turned out to be true, and one item that turned out to be false.

1. Write on the blackboard:

ALL 3—IN COMMON (THE SAME)

2. Tell the students something that you had heard about another country or city (or the city you are currently in, if you are from somewhere else) that turned out not to be true, and write it on the blackboard, such as:

Before I went to France, I <u>had heard</u> that French people were not very friendly to Americans, but they were very friendly to me.

Give another example, this time of something that turned out to be true, and write it on the blackboard:

I <u>had also heard</u> that people spoke very fast. This was true! I could hardly understand anybody when I was there.

3. Give each group the following instructions:

> Discuss some of the things that you had heard about the United States (or the English-speaking country in which you are studying) before you arrived. (If you are not in an English-speaking country now, talk about the city, school, or class in which you are studying.) Which of these things turned out to be true, and which turned out to be false?
>
> As you talk together, try to find at least one thing that <u>all three</u> of you had heard that turned out to be true, and one that turned out to be false. You all must agree on whether your ideas are true after all, or not.

Accountability: Have a member of each group report its findings to the class. Write the first set of answers on the blackboard to serve as a model for subsequent reports from other groups.

                    Be prepared to ignore the accuracy of tense shifts in reported speech, unless your students have already worked on these structures. For example, most students will say, *We had heard people <u>are</u> . . .*, rather than <u>*were*</u> . . . .

PAST PERFECT CONTINUOUS

Theme: Searching for things (Imagination)

Group Size: Pairs

Goal: Decide how long a person had been looking for an item.

1. Write on the blackboard:

   STATEMENT: On _____, Janet found _____.
                (yesterday's date)   (One of the items on blackboard)

a yellow umbrella	a blue bird	a job
a used bicycle	a new jacket	a rich husband
a parking space	a house (an apartment)	a red scarf

   MINUTES HOURS DAYS WEEKS MONTHS YEARS

   QUESTION: How long had Janet been looking for _____ when she found one?

2. Ask a student to read the statement from the blackboard. (You have already filled in yesterday's date and an item from the list.) Have another student ask the question from the blackboard, filling in the item from the statement. Help the first student answer the question, using a time word from the blackboard.

3. Erase the item from the statement on the blackboard and replace it with another item. Demonstrate with two new students, preferably from opposite sides of the room to make the alternating roles clearer. Have the first student read the statement and the second ask the question. Again, help the first student to respond using the time words from the blackboard, such as, *She had been looking for a parking space for twenty minutes (when she found one).*

4. Give each pair the following instructions:

   > Take turns making statements and asking and answering questions about each item on the blackboard. One partner should choose an item and put it into the statement about when Janet found it. The other partner should ask the question about how long Janet had been looking. Then the first partner should answer, using one of the time words from the blackboard. Use all the words on the blackboard; then add some of your own.

Accountability: After a few minutes, erase the models from the blackboard, then circulate. At the end of the activity, ask a few students for random answers to the *How long?* question. Then have a few volunteer pairs present their original statements and answers to the class.

Variation: Extend this activity by erasing the blackboard and using different topics, such as: *How long had Kevin been using his old _____ when it finally broke?*

TV	camera	bicycle	suitcase
watch	radio	typewriter	umbrella

PAST PERFECT CONTINUOUS

Theme: Interruptions (Imagination)

Group Size: Pairs

Goal: Guess what happened based on what a partner says he or she had been doing.

1. Write on the blackboard (choose about ten of these that might apply to your students)

    . . . WHEN . . .

. . . the school bell rang	. . . the alarm clock went off
. . . the phone rang	. . . the rooster woke me up
. . . the teacher told us to stop	. . . the car broke down
. . . the rain began	. . . the train arrived
. . . someone came to the door	. . . the teacher entered the room
. . . it got dark	. . . the sun came up
. . . the electricity went off	. . . my partner fell asleep

    $\left\{ \begin{matrix} \text{We} \\ \text{I} \end{matrix} \right\}$ had been _____ing for _____ $\left\{ \begin{matrix} \text{minutes} \\ \text{hours} \end{matrix} \right\}$ when _____.

2. Give each pair the following instruction:

    > One of you will be Partner A and the other Partner B. Partner A should choose one of the events on the blackboard. Let's say, for example, that you chose . . . *the train arrived.* Then think of something that you can tell Partner B you <u>had already been doing</u> when the train arrived. It should be some activity that will help Partner B guess which event you chose. For example, if you say, *I had been waiting for forty-five minutes . . .,* Partner B will not be able to guess, but if you say, *I had been waiting in the station for forty-five minutes,* your partner will be able to guess the answer more easily. Follow the model on the blackboard. Partner A will only give the first half of the sentence and Partner B will guess the second half.
    >
    > After each completed sentence, exchange roles. Keep working until you have completed all the events on the blackboard.

3. Start the activity by playing the role of Partner A yourself. You will probably need more than one practice example to make it clear. Wait for the answer (event) you had in mind for each example, so that the students will do the same. For example, if you chose . . . *it got dark* and you say, *I had been reading a book outside under a tree for two hours when . . .,* and a students says, . . . *it started to rain,* acknowledge the answer as a good possibility, but not the one you had in mind.

Accountability: At the end of the activity, call on the students for sample answers to some of the examples on the blackboard.

FUTURE PERFECT

Theme: Naughty children (Imagination)

Group Size: Four to five students

Goal: Prepare clever ideas to share with the class.

1. Put on the blackboard:

eat

break

drop

open

paint

What will the children have done by the time the Smiths get back?

2. Tell the students about the Smith family:

> This is the Smith family. Mr. and Mrs. Smith have three children: Johnny, age 7; Billy, age 5; and Winnie, age 3. They are going out to dinner and to the theater tonight, so they will be back home very late. They have hired a babysitter, Susan, to take care of the children. But they do not know that Susan is very, very tired, and she is going to fall asleep on the living-room sofa soon after the Smiths leave. She will not wake up until the Smiths come back. What do you think the children will have done by the time the Smiths return?

3. Give each group the following instructions:

> Discuss what each of the three children will have done by the time their parents return. Use your imagination and action verbs like the ones on the blackboard, in your description. Make sure that all of the actions are completed and use the future perfect tense, such as, *Winnie will have poured all the milk from the refrigerator onto the floor.*
>
> Write one of your group's ideas on the blackboard, and be prepared to tell the class another one.

Accountability: Have someone from each group read the group's answer from the board, and have another group member give an idea orally. (The sentences should have been written on the blackboard while the groups were still talking.)

         Be prepared for some students to give answers that would be more appropriate in the future continuous tense (for things that the children will still be doing), or in the simple future tense (for stative verbs). For example, someone might say, *The children will have slept.* or *The children will have been tired.* You might suggest completed action alternatives for these sentences such as *The children will have fallen asleep,* or *become tired.*

FUTURE PERFECT

Theme: Students' futures (Imagination)

Group Size: Whole class (individuals circulating)

Goal: Find out what year is on one's own back based on information received from other students.

Materials: Scrap paper and a straight pin for each student

1. Write on the blackboard:

2000	2010	2020	2030	2040	2050	get married	get divorced
						retire	buy
						sell	meet
						finish	move
						graduate	start
						change	make

2. Ask a student volunteer to come to the front of the class. Pin to his or her back a large scrap of paper with the year *2020* written on it. The class should see the number, but the student volunteer should not. Tell the student that he or she must guess which year (from those written on the blackboard) is written on his or her back, based on what you say.

3. Write on the blackboard and tell the student two or three things that you think might have happened to that student by that year; for example:

    You <u>will have graduated</u> from college by that year.

    You <u>probably will have moved</u> to a big city by that year.

    You <u>will have found</u> a job by that year.

    Let the class help you with additional sentence cues until the student guesses the year. Encourage the students to use only the words on the blackboard (because they more or less guarantee a completed action, which is required by the future perfect tense).

4. Repeat the model by letting students put a year on <u>your</u> back. Try to guess it from the students' sentence cues.

5. Have each student choose one of the future years from the blackboard and write it on a scrap of paper, letting no one see it. Then, have each student pin that year on the back of another student, making sure that no one sees what year is on his or her own back.

6. Give the class the following instructions:

> Move from person to person, looking at each student's back to see the year. Tell each person what he or she will (or might) have done, or what will have happened to that person, by that year. As you listen to what your classmates tell you about <u>your</u> future, try to guess what year is written on your back. When you think you know, come up and tell me.

Accountability: When students have guessed the year, they should come and tell you so that you can verify their guesses.

To verify accuracy during the activity, participate in it yourself. To help ensure accuracy, since the future perfect tense is so dependent on the choice of verb, you might want to provide additional suggested verbs on the blackboard in order to avoid confusion with the future continuous (unfinished activity) and simple future (stative verb) tenses.

FUTURE PERFECT

Theme: A baby's future (Imagination)

Group Size: Four or five students

Goal: Prepare sentences to present to the class about a baby's future at five different ages.

1. Put on the blackboard:

Pamela  learn how to

finish

3 months start doing

stop doing

WILL + HAVE + past participle

2. Tell the students that the baby on the board is Pamela, who is three months old. They are going to predict her future.

3. Give each group the following instructions:

> Choose five different ages in Pamela's future (up to and including 21 years old), and decide what she will have learned how to do, finished, started doing, or stopped doing by the time she reaches each of the ages you have chosen. For example, if the first age you choose is *six months*, you might say, *By the age of six months, Pamela will have learned how to sit up.* (Write on the blackboard.) If you choose *six years*, you might say, *By the age of six, she probably will have started going to school.* You should have several ideas for each age you choose and be prepared to tell them to the class.

Accountability: Have a member of each group present one or two sentences to the class, and write some of them on the blackboard to reinforce the pattern. Have the class determine whether each idea is feasible.

FUTURE PERFECT CONTINUOUS

Theme: Students' futures (Imagination)

Group Size: Pairs

Goal: Based on what a partner says about how long he or she has been studying English, figure out when that person expects some future event to happen.

1. Write on the blackboard (or vary as appropriate for your class):

get married	graduate from . . .	buy a house
find a great job	retire	reach the age of . . .

   By the time I graduate from this school, I <u>will have been studying</u> English for eight years.

   By the time I get married, I probably <u>will have been studying English</u> for thirty years!

2. Tell the class the following:

   I have news for you. You are all going to be studying English for the rest of your lives. Why not? I am still studying it, and it is my own language. But you will also be doing other things, although you may not be exactly sure when. Try to decide, in any case, in what year you think you might be doing the things I have listed on the blackboard. Do you remember when you began studying English?

3. Give each pair the following instructions:

   > Using the model sentences on the blackboard as guides, tell your partner how long you will have been studying English by the time each of the events on the blackboard takes place in your life. You also need to tell your partner when you began studying English. Your partner will then figure out when you plan for each future event to happen. After you have talked about four or five events in your future, exchange roles with your partner and talk about his or her future.

Accountability: For each item on the blackboard, ask a student about his or her partner.

FUTURE PERFECT CONTINUOUS

Theme: Student abilities and activities (Real information exchange)

Group Size: Pairs

Goal: Based on what a partner says, figure out when that person began doing a certain activity.

Materials: Scrap paper for each student.

1. Write on the blackboard (the three items below should apply to yourself):

   3 things you know how to do and plan to do for the rest of your life:

   ride a bicycle every day   cook   study foreign languages

   By the year 2020, I <u>will have been riding</u> a bicycle every day for thirty-seven years!

2. Tell the class the following:

   By the year 2020, I will have been riding a bicycle every day for thirty-seven years. When did I start doing this? (Allow students to answer.)

   By the year 2020, I will have been cooking for fifty-two years. When did I start cooking? (Again, wait for the answer.)

   By the year 2020, I will have been studying foreign languages for sixty-six years! When did I start? (Wait for the answer.)

3. Ask the students each to think of three activities that they do now—sports, music, jobs, hobbies, and so on—that they plan to be doing for the rest of their lives. Give them at least four or five minutes to think.

4. On a scrap of paper, have the students write down the year that they began doing each of these activities, and then subtract that year from 2020. (You might want to demonstrate with one of your own examples on the blackboard.) Tell them they will be using this number in the sentences they will be forming.

5. Give each pair the following instructions:

   > Tell your partner about each of your three activities, one at a time. Follow the model on the blackboard and inform him or her of how long you will have been doing this activity by the year 2020. Your partner should guess the year you started. After you have discussed all three of your activities, exchange roles.

Accountability: Ask each student about one of his or her partner's activities. Have the class guess and verify the starting year.

PRESENT REAL CONDITIONAL

Theme: Presents and prizes (Imagination)

Group Size: Pairs

Goal: Try to think of unusual things to do with unusual gifts.

1. Write on the blackboard:

    a very large chocolate elephant

    (results of brainstorming with class)

2. Brainstorm with the class at least ten other unusual gifts or prizes that a person might receive, and write them on the blackboard.

3. Give each pair the following instructions:

    > Ask your partner questions about two or three of the items on the blackboard, following the model question (write on the blackboard):
    >
    > If I give you a _____, what will you do with it?
    >
    > Write one of your partner's answers on the blackboard, preferably the most unusual or interesting one.

4. Before letting the students begin the activity, review the verb tenses in the model question. After students have been working on the activity for a few minutes, erase the model.

Accountability: Review the sentences that the students have written on the blackboard and make corrections.

PRESENT REAL CONDITIONAL

Theme: Silly prizes (Imagination)

Group Size: Pairs

Goal: Decide what to do with each prize.

1. Put on the blackboard:

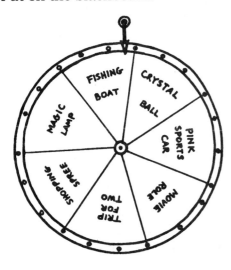

   1. Trip for two to Antarctica

   2. Pink sports car

   3. Crystal ball

   4. Fishing boat in the Aral Sea

   5. "Member of the crowd" role in a new movie

   6. Magic lamp (with genie)

   7. One-week shopping spree on Mt. Everest

   If we win the _____, we will _____.

   OPTIONS: keep and use, give away, refuse and take cash value

2. Tell the students that they have just won a spin at this big wheel. This means that they will <u>definitely</u> get one of the prizes, but they do not yet know which one it will be. Each pair of students wins one prize.

3. Give each pair the following instructions:

   > Discuss each of the possible prizes with your partner, and decide what you will do with each one of them if you win it. If you decide to keep and use the prize, be prepared to tell the class what you will do with it. If you don't want the prize, decide if you will give it away, and to whom, or if you will refuse it and take the cash value, whatever it is.

4. Before beginning the activity, review the list of prizes to make sure that the students understand what they might win.

Accountability: Have each pair tell the class what they will do with the prize that you randomly point to on the wheel (for each pair).

Variation: Conclude with a kind of "pin the tail on the donkey" activity for each pair to find out what they have really won. Blindfold one student in each pair, turn him or her around three times, and head the student in the direction of the wheel with an extended finger to select the pair's prize.

PRESENT REAL CONDITIONAL

Theme: Things people will never do (Real information exchange)

Group Size: Three to four students

Goal: Agree on something that no one in the group will ever do.

1. Write on the blackboard:

       $50,000   NEVER!

2. Tell the students something that you will never do, even if someone offers you $50,000 to do it. Write a sentence about it on the blackboard, for example:

   Even if someone offers me $50,000, I will never jump out of an airplane with a parachute.

3. Give each group the following instructions:

   > Find at least one thing that no one in your group will ever do, even if someone offers you $50,000 to do it. You may find more than one of these things, but they all <u>have to be</u> things that some people actually do.

Accountability: Have one member of each group report to the class. Note the new item on the blackboard. After everyone has reported, get a show of hands to find out the things that no one in the whole class (if possible) will ever do.

PRESENT UNREAL CONDITIONAL

Theme: Classroom improvement (Imagination)

Group Size: Five students

Goal: List items in a plan on the blackboard, with projected costs.

1. Write on the blackboard:

	IF	+	simple past
$5,000	WOULD	+	simple form

2. Ask the students to look around the classroom and tell you if they think it is perfect, or if it could use some improvement. Tell them that you are going to give them $5,000 to improve the classroom.

3. Give the students an example of your own and write it on the blackboard, such as:

   If I had $5,000 to spend, first I would buy a new teacher's desk and a stool with a big, soft cushion on top.

   Leave the model on the blackboard until the activity is well underway, and then erase it.

4. Give each group the following instructions:

   > Discuss what you would do with $5,000 to fix up the classroom if you had the money. Do not spend it all on one thing. Plan to use the money for at least five different items or groups of items. Estimate the cost for each item, including the labor, unless your group is willing to do the labor yourselves (such as painting). You will have to use the verb form *would* in your discussion, because I am not really ever going to give you the money.
   >
   > Once you have made your plans for spending all the money, put a list of the things you are going to do and buy on the blackboard, including how much you think each item will cost.

Accountability: Have a member of each group come up to the blackboard and describe their plans, using the notes on the blackboard and the correct tenses.

Variation: Instead of announcing a $5,000 budget, have the students decide how much money they think would be required in order to fix up the classroom nicely, and use that amount as a budget for this activity.

PRESENT UNREAL CONDITIONAL

Theme: Student problems (Imagination)

Group Size: Whole class (individuals circulating)

Goal: Figure out the problem written on one's back based on advice given by classmates.

Materials: Scrap paper and a straight pin for each student

1. Write on the blackboard:

    1 problem   If I were you I'd _____

2. Brainstorm a few very specific problems that any student in the class might have at some time (a stolen car, a broken arm, a troublesome sibling, too much work, and so on) and write them on the blackboard.

3. Ask each student to imagine <u>one</u> single problem that any one of the students in the class might have. Tell each student to write the problem <u>legibly</u> on a piece of paper and not let anyone see it, then pin the paper on the back of a classmate, and make sure that that classmate does not see what is written.

4. In order to prevent the students from writing a list of problems rather than just one problem (because some more ambitious or imaginative students often interpret one as a minimum rather than as a specific requirement), you might want to draw a large scrap of paper on the blackboard containing one problem written in large letters, which takes up most of the paper.

5. Give the class the following instructions:

    > Walk around the room and look at the tags on one another's backs. Each time you read a person's problem, give that person a piece of related advice, using the form, *If I were you, I'd* . . . Your advice would help that person solve the problem, but do not be very specific, because you do not want him or her to guess the problem too easily. For example, if the problem is <u>Stolen car</u>, do not say, *If I were you I'd tell the police about my car.* Rather, say, *If I were you, I'd report it to the police.*
    >
    > Each person should need to hear several pieces of advice before guessing his or her problem. When you think you have guessed what your own problem is, come tell me and show me your back. I will take off your tag, and you can return to the class and continue to give advice until everyone has guessed his or her problem.

Accountability: As each student tells you his or her problem, ask what piece of advice revealed the answer. Prizes for the first ones done make this activity even livelier.

PRESENT UNREAL CONDITIONAL

Theme: Housesitting (Imagination/role play)

Group Size: Six students

Goal: Give truthful answers about what one would do within a role play situation. Sally must make a choice.

1. Draw on the blackboard (make these figures represent your class as accurately as possible in terms of gender):

2. Tell the students that the woman on the blackboard is Sally, who is a very organized, careful, rich, and smart young woman. She lives in a large and beautiful house in the mountains of California, where there are frequent fires, earthquakes, and landslides. (Explain vocabulary here.) She is going away on a trip around the world for six months, and she is looking for someone to take care of her house while she is gone. The people on the blackboard around Sally are being interviewed for the job.

3. Have the members of each group choose a role to play according to the pictures on the blackboard. One student should be Sally, and each of the other five should choose a person being interviewed to role-play.

4. Give each group the following instructions:

> Sally is going to ask each person in your group some questions about what he or she would do in certain situations, or if certain things happened, while she was away. She should ask each person in the group the same questions, listening carefully to their answers, because she must choose one member of the group to take care of her house while she is away. For example, if Sally asks the first person, *What would you do if the electricity went off?* or *What would you do if it rained hard for four days and you heard about landslides nearby?*, she must also ask the four other members of your group the same question.
>
> Group members should try to give truthful answers—what do you think you really would do in these situations?

Accountability: Have each "Sally" tell who she has chosen to take care of her house and why, describing that person's answers to her questions.

Variation: You might want to use a different scenario, such as a young man or young woman trying to choose a mate, or change Sally's locale from California to closer to home.

PRESENT UNREAL CONDITIONAL

Theme: Aliens from outer space

Group Size: Five students

Goal: Agree on at least three recommendations for the planet Earth.

1. Put on the blackboard:

ALIEN

2. Give each group the following instructions:

> If you were aliens from a superior planet and you had complete control over the planet Earth, what would you do? What would you change and what would you leave the same? How would you make the changes? Agree on at least three recommendations to report to the Space Council. Remember to use *would* in your discussion, since this situation is not really going to happen. . . or is it??

Accountability: Set up a "Space Council" of three students to which each group will report. Have one member of each group list its three recommendations on the blackboard (in note form), and have another member of that group describe the plan using appropriate conditional forms. Vote together on the three best recommendations.

PAST UNREAL CONDITIONAL

Theme: Fate (Real information exchange)

Group Size: Four students

Goal: Decide which story is the most dramatic or pivotal in a student's life to share with the class.

1. Write on the blackboard:

    LUCKY !!

2. Ask the students to think of something lucky that happened to them in the past—preferably something that had an important effect on their lives. You might want to brainstorm a little on the subject of lucky events (accidental meetings, being late or early, getting lost or taking a wrong route, finding or losing something, and so on) and write ideas on the blackboard in order to get the activity started.

3. Give the students a model from your own experience and write it on the blackboard before giving instructions for the activity. For example:

    If my car <u>had not broken down</u> on February 5, 1978, I <u>would not have met</u> my husband.

    If my husband <u>had not been</u> early for an appointment, he <u>might not have stopped</u> to help me.

4. Give each group the following instructions:

    > Tell the other people in your group how your life would (or might) have been different if a certain event or accident in your life had not happened. You may need to explain a little about what happened before making your final statement about how your life would have been different. For example, you might need to explain that you were walking down the street one day and you heard someone call you from behind. You stopped and turned around to try to hear what the person was saying. Because you stopped, you did not get hit by the truck that was speeding out of control right where you were going to walk. If you had not stopped to listen, you would have been hit by the truck.
    >
    > Be sure to finish your description with a conditional sentence; use the model on the blackboard. Your group may also help you think of other ways your life might have been different if things had happened differently.
    >
    > When everyone in your group has told his or her story, decide together which story is the most dramatic.

Accountability: Have each group report its members' most dramatic story. Conclude the activity by having the class complete the following sentence on the blackboard:

    If we had not come to class today, . . .

Variation: <u>Unlucky</u> events instead.

PAST UNREAL CONDITIONAL

Theme: Life in the Stone Age (Imagination)

Group Size: Four or five students of the same gender

Goal: Write a few ideas on the blackboard.

1. Write on the blackboard:

10,000 years ago

2. Give each group the following instructions:

> Discuss how your life would have been different if you had lived 10,000 years ago. Also discuss ways in which you think your life would have been the same as it is now. Female groups should try to focus on the lives of women, and male groups on the lives of men, but this is not absolutely necessary.

3. Before letting the groups begin, say and write an example or two on the blackboard to set the pattern. (You may want to brainstorm facts and vocabulary about living conditions for prehistoric people, depending on the sophistication of your class.) Erase the model(s) after the groups have been talking for a few minutes. For example:

   If I <u>had lived</u> 10,000 years ago, I <u>would have spoken</u> a different language, and I <u>would not have known</u> how to write.

   If I <u>had lived</u> 10,000 years ago, I <u>wouldn't have seen</u> an airplane, a car, or even a plow!

Accountability: As the groups are discussing their ideas they should send representatives to the blackboard to write any particularly good ideas that they come up with. You may want to walk around and listen for these good ideas during the activity, asking students to go to the blackboard when you hear them.

                    When the group discussions are over, have the whole class look at the sentences on the blackboard and try to determine whether they were written by male or female groups. The success of this process will be determined largely by the nature of gender roles in the students' current society(ies). If things have not changed too much, and/or if your class is either all-male or all-female, you might want to eliminate this stage of the activity. On the other hand, the class also might discuss the extent to which gender roles have changed in their culture(s).

Variation: Have the students discuss <u>similarities only</u> between modern life and prehistoric life. In this case, you may have to remind your class about the word *still*, as in *If I had lived 10,000 years ago, I still would have worried about my future.*

PAST UNREAL CONDITIONAL

Theme: History (Imagination)

Group Size: Pairs

Goal: Write a sentence on the blackboard about how history might have been
                  different.

1. Write on the blackboard (or choose some other event in history that your class knows):

    If the French Revolution had not happened, Napoleon would not have come to power.

2. Give each pair the following instructions:

    > Think of an important event in world history. Decide how history (or life now)
    > might have been different (or would have been different) if that event had not
    > happened. Discuss as many events as you have time for, and write your condi-
    > tional sentences on the blackboard.

Accountability: Examine the sentences on the blackboard for accuracy and have the class
                      agree or disagree with the assertions.

Variation: If your class is older, somewhat sophisticated, and ethnically diverse, you
                      might want to group the students according to countries of origin and have
                      them describe how their countries might have been different if some particu-
                      lar historical event had not happened.

WISH (PRESENT OR FUTURE)

Theme: Wishes (Imagination)

Group Size: Pairs

Goal: Perform original dialogue in front of the class from memory.

Materials: Scrap paper for notes (optional)

1. Draw on the blackboard:

2. Give each pair the following instructions:

> Complete the dialogue on the blackboard. Do not write it out. You may write down a few notes to help you remember, but try to memorize your actual complete dialogue as you prepare it to present to the class. Please check your last two dialogue balloons with me so that I can make sure they are correct.

Accountability: Take notes as the pairs present their conversations, and review the errors when everyone is done. Be prepared for some students to require *would* in the last dialogue balloon (as in *I wish you would appreciate what you have.*) in the sense of *having the willingness to do something.*

WISH (PRESENT OR FUTURE)

Theme: The way things ought to be (Imagination)

Group Size: Four to five students

Goal: Share the more original ideas with the class.

1. Write on the blackboard:

   geography   weather   life   laws of physics

   a. I wish people could fly without airplanes.

   b. I wish New York and California were much closer together.

   c. I wish summers were less hot.

   d. I wish all people had enough to eat.

2. Tell the students to look at the sentences on the blackboard and decide which sentence matches which of the categories above (a = laws of physics; b = geography; c = weather; d = life). Make sure that the students understand the categories before beginning the activity.

3. Give each group the following instructions:

   > Choose a category from the blackboard (or a similar category of your own) and discuss how you wish that things were different than they actually are. Be ready to tell the rest of the class some of your ideas. Each group should write at least one idea on the blackboard in a complete sentence.

Accountability: After you review the sentences already on the blackboard (and correct any errors), have a member of each group present more of that group's ideas. Let the class decide which category each idea falls into and see if their decision matches the category that the group originally selected.

WISH + WOULD (PRESENT OR FUTURE)

Theme: World politics and problems (Imagination)

Group Size: Whole class (individuals circulating)

Goal: Express wishes about how certain people or organizations could make the world better.

1. Write on the blackboard:

   powerful person   country   organization

   I wish _____ would _____.

2. Ask each student to think of <u>one</u> powerful person, country, or organization that he or she thinks is important enough to change the world in some way. (Examples: the United States government, the United Nations, OPEC, the European Community, the Prime Minister of Japan, and so on.)

3. Give the class the following instructions:

   > Talk to many different students in the class. Tell each student the name of the person, country, or organization you thought of. That student should tell you what he or she wishes that person or group would do to change the world. Follow the model on the blackboard. For example, if you tell me that your choice is the United Nations, I might say, *I wish the United Nations would try harder to save the environment.*
   >
   > If a student you talk to does not recognize the name of your person, country, or organization, you should explain it to him or her.
   >
   > Try to remember any interesting answers you hear.

Accountability: Ask the students to volunteer their more interesting answers. Write some of them on the blackboard in the correct form.

WISH (PAST)

Theme: Life's mistakes (Real information exchange)

Group Size: Three to five students

Goal: Keep score as to the number of regrets expressed by one's whole group.

1. Write on the blackboard:

    this morning   this past year

    last weekend   in the past five years

    last week   in the past ten years

    last year   when you were much younger

    This morning I got up at 8:00.

    I wish I had gotten up at 7:00.

2. Give each group the following instructions:

    > Think of some things that you did wrong, or that you should have done but did
    > not do at all, during the times shown on the blackboard. Choose any of the
    > times and tell your group what you did or did not do; then, tell them what you
    > wish you had done or had not done. Follow the model on the blackboard.
    >   You may also want to tell your group why you wish you had done something
    > differently. For example, using the model on the blackboard, I might say, *I could
    > have done more work.*
    >   Be sure to use past modals for past regrets. Keep a count of the number of
    > regrets expressed in your group.

Accountability: Find out which group has the most regrets, and which one has the fewest.
                    Have a member of each of those groups tell the class some of those regrets.
                    Write some of them on the blackboard.

Variation: Instead of counting the total number of regrets in each group, have each
                    group try to find things that all of its members regret. In this case, groups of
                    three are better, as it is easier to find common items in a smaller group. For
                    accountability, while the groups tell how many common regrets they have, or
                    what their common regrets are, try to find a regret common to the whole
                    class (including you, the teacher).

WISH (PAST)

Theme: Past mistakes (Imagination)

Group Size: Three to five students

Goal: Create one sentence using *wish* for each category on the blackboard.

1. Put on the blackboard:

family

friends

career/work

school

travel

shopping

2. Tell the students the following:

> This is Mrs. Bradshaw. She is a very happy and successful lawyer with three grown children and a wonderful, loving husband. Her life has been very good. But it has not been perfect. She has made a few mistakes in her life, so she wishes that she had done some things differently.

3. Give each group the following instructions:

> Think of a mistake that Mrs. Bradshaw made in each of the categories on the blackboard. Then, create a sentence that tells what she wishes she <u>had done</u> instead of what she really did do. For example, if you choose <u>friends</u>, you might say, *Mrs. Bradshaw wishes she had written more letters and made more telephone calls to her friends over the years (during her life).* (Write on the blackboard.)
>
> Try to create a *wish* sentence for at least three categories.

Accountability: As the groups are working, walk around the room and listen for good answers. As you hear them, have a student from the group write the sentence(s) on the blackboard. Try to get two examples for each category. When everyone is done, review the sentences and correct them on the blackboard.

WISH (PAST)

Theme: World events

Group Size: Three students

Goal: Create a wish list that would change the world.

1. Write on the blackboard (spread the categories out across the top):

   environment   inventions   famous people   natural and historical events

   a. I wish rock and roll had never been invented.

   b. I wish William Shakespeare had written more plays.

   c. I wish the forests of Europe and America had not been cut down.

   d. I wish the World Wars had never happened.

   (If possible, choose something historical and close to your students' lives, rather than such a general statement.)

2. Tell the students to look at the sentences on the blackboard and decide which one goes with which category (a = inventions; b = famous people; c = environment; d = natural and historical events).

3. Have the students each choose one of the categories on the blackboard and form a group with two other students who have chosen the same category.

4. Give each group the following instructions:

   > Discuss events in your category which each of you wishes had never happened. Try to find at least one event that all three of you agree should never have happened, and prepare to share it with the rest of the class. Create a *wish* sentence like the ones on the blackboard, and remember to put your verb into the past perfect tense to express a wish about the past. Write each of your ideas in note form on the blackboard under the appropriate category.

Accountability: After each group has written at least one item on the blackboard, go through each item and ask which group wrote it. Have a member of that group give a complete sentence that expresses the group's wish about that category.

Sample response for the category *inventions:* gunpowder

Student sentence: We wish gunpowder had not been invented.

MODALS: *COULD / MAY / MIGHT*

Theme: Proverbs (Imagination)

Group Size: Five students

Goal: Find the correct answer.

1. Write on the blackboard:

(a proverb of your choice, but one whose meaning may not be so obvious, yet whose vocabulary is straightforward and simple, such as the following:

A bird in the hand is worth two in the bush.

People who live in glass houses should not throw stones.

Don't judge a book by its cover.

IT MIGHT MEAN . . .   IT MAY MEAN . . .   IT COULD MEAN . . .

2. Give each group the following instructions:

> Try to guess what the saying (proverb) on the blackboard means. Use *could,* *may,* and *might* as you make your suggestions. If you have trouble getting started, or if you need help as you go, send a spy or two to some other group(s) for ideas. Write your best guess on the blackboard, using *could, may,* or *might.*

Accountability: The students' sentences on the blackboard will verify accuracy. Make any necessary corrections, then circle the guess that is closest to the real meaning of the proverb. Explain the real meaning.

      Have students determine whether their own language has a similar proverb, and ask them to translate that proverb literally into English for the class.

MODALS: COULD / MAY / MIGHT

Theme: Reasons behind feelings and expressions (Imagination)

Group Size: Three to five students

Goal: Prepare a reason for what each figure on the blackboard is doing.

1. Put on the blackboard:

looking out the window

barking   crying   smiling   frowning   laughing

It $\begin{Bmatrix} \text{could} \\ \text{might} \\ \text{may} \end{Bmatrix}$ want to go out.

She $\begin{Bmatrix} \text{could} \\ \text{might} \\ \text{may} \end{Bmatrix}$ be dreaming about her vacation in Tahiti.

2. Tell the students the following:

> This is the Nelson family. The dog is barking, the baby is crying, the girl is smiling and sleeping, the boy is looking out the window, the father is frowning, and the mother is laughing. We do not know why. For example, we do not know why the father is frowning, or why the dog is barking.

3. Give each group the following instructions:

> Discuss what you think could (may/might) be the reason why the people (and the dog) in the picture are doing what they are doing. Use *could, may,* and *might* to express your ideas about the possible reasons, referring to the models on the blackboard to form your sentences. After a few minutes, however, I will erase those models.

Accountability: Point to each figure in the picture and call on representatives from several different groups to give their ideas about each figure as you are indicating it. Do one figure at a time, writing sample answers on the blackboard as you go.

MODALS: *COULD / MAY / MIGHT*

Theme: Disturbing the peace (Imagination)

Group Size: Three to four students

Goal: Think of neighborhood noises that might keep a person from taking a peaceful afternoon nap.

1. Put on the blackboard:

Mrs. Peters

2. Tell the students the following story:

> This is Mrs. Peters. She has just moved into a new neighborhood, and she is very happy there except for one thing. She likes to take a short rest in the afternoon, but in her new house it is impossible because of all the noises that people are making around her house. Dogs, trucks, city workers, children, neighbors, and even the neighborhood cats are keeping her awake.

3. Give each group the following instructions:

> Discuss what you think the people, the animals, and the machines around Mrs. Peters could/may/might be doing that keep her awake. Be creative. Make your examples unusual or funny if you want.

4. Start the activity off by giving your own example and writing it on the blackboard, such as:

   Her neighbor could / might / may be building a doghouse in the backyard.

Accountability: Ask one member of each group to tell the class its most interesting example. Since this activity elicits the continuous form of the verb following the modal, you might want to write a few students' answers on the blackboard, especially if the forms need some correction.

Variation: Draw a bus on the blackboard, and tell the class the following: This is Jon. He is riding the bus on a long trip between _____ and _____. (Choose two cities your students know.) He brought a book with him to read, but he cannot read because of the children in the seat behind him. I am not sure what they are doing.
     Tell the groups to think of things that the children might be doing to disturb Jon.

MODALS: *COULD / MAY / MIGHT*

Theme: Road and traffic signs (Real information exchange)

Group Size: Three to five students

Goal: Guess the logic behind the colors used in road signs in the United States.

1. Put on the blackboard:

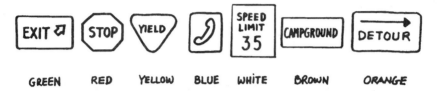

Red could mean . . .   White might mean . . .   Yellow may mean . . .

2. Brainstorm with the class additional examples of road and traffic signs in each of the
   various colors, and write the ideas on the blackboard under the appropriate signs. Outside
   the United States, add the items listed below to your blackboard preparation. (Or, if you
   prefer, use the color or shape coding system for the country you are in.

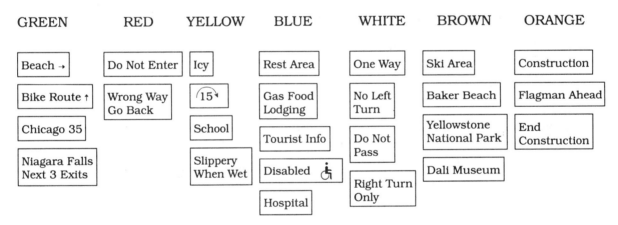

3. Give each group the following instructions:

   > Try to figure out the meaning behind the different colors used for traffic and
   > road signs. Use *could, may,* and *might* to offer suggestions.

Accountability: One at a time, point to each sample sign on the blackboard and ask for
volunteers to suggest possible meanings for the color. As the students zero
in on the correct meanings, write them on the blackboard, but without a
modal (for example, *Red means danger*).

   green—directions   white—regulations
   red—danger   brown—parks and recreation
   yellow—warning, caution   orange—temporary
   blue—services

MODALS: MAY / MIGHT VS. MUST

Theme: Nations and languages (Real information exchange)

Group Size: Whole class

Goal: Determine what language(s) a person from a given country *must* speak, and what he *may or might* speak.

1. Put on the blackboard:

PORTUGAL

He *must* speak Portuguese.

He $\left\{ \begin{array}{l} \text{may} \\ \underline{\text{might}} \end{array} \right\}$ speak Spanish.

2. Tell the class the following:

> This boy lives in Portugal. We can be 99% sure that he speaks Portuguese. In other words, he *must* speak Portuguese (indicate first sentence on blackboard). But since Portugal is located right next to Spain, and Spanish is related to Portuguese, it is also *possible* that he knows Spanish, so he *may* speak Spanish (indicate second sentence on blackboard).

3. Erase *Portugal* and the sentences about Portuguese and Spanish. Write *Mexico* on the blackboard.

4. Give the class the following instructions:

> Tell me about this boy. He lives in Mexico. What language are you almost sure that he speaks? What languages might he speak?

5. Continue the activity by erasing and substituting country names appropriate for your group. (You might also choose a more appropriate model for #2 above if your students are not familiar with Portugal.)

Accountability: As a whole-class activity, verification of student accuracy is built into this exercise.

Variation: Substitute *like to eat* or *live near* for the verb *speak* to generate different sentences.

MODALS: MUST (INFERENCE)

Theme: Occupations

Group Size: Whole class

Goal: Guess an occupation based on the pantomime of another student.

1. Write on the blackboard:

YOU MUST BE A(N). . .

doctor	musician	auto mechanic	cowboy
pilot	typist	farmer	dressmaker/tailor
waiter	teacher	athlete	actor/actress
painter	carpenter	scientist	astronaut
soldier	artist	dancer	movie director
fisherman	hunter	author	cashier
salesperson	ship captain	bus driver	circus performer

2. Give the class the following instructions:

> Choose one of the occupations on the blackboard. When it is your turn, come to the front of the class and, without speaking, show the class something that a person in that occupation does as part of his or her job. Anyone in the class who can guess what you are doing and what your job is should raise a hand and say, *You must be a(n) . . .* with the name of the occupation. Whoever guesses the answer can act out the next occupation.
> I will start. (Demonstrate a painter painting.)

Accountability: As a whole-class activity, the accountability is built in.

Variation: You can divide a very large class into two or three groups and have them sit in circles. In this case, however, the students may be inclined to stay seated while they do the pantomime, seriously limiting their actions. Therefore, it is best to encourage the students to stand while they pantomime. To verify accuracy, you can circulate among the groups.

Large groups are better for this activity, because everyone then has plenty of time to think and no one has to pantomime too much. Shy students need not be forced to participate; volunteers can substitute for them.

MODALS: MUST (INFERENCE)

Theme: Happiness and health

Group Size: Four to five students

Goal: Discuss and try to agree about which of two situations is better.

1. Put on the blackboard:

PAIR 1	PAIR 2	PAIR 3

A. rich	B. poor	A. works hard	B. works little	A. doctor	B. doctor
no children	four healthy children	eats mostly vegetables	eats plenty of meat	cures the poor for free	very rich
Who must be happier?		Who must be healthier?		Who must be more satisfied with his life?	

2. Give each group the following instructions:

> Discuss the six people on the blackboard, one pair at a time. Decide which person in each pair must be in the better situation. That is, for Pair 1, decide who must be happier; for Pair 2, decide who must be healthier; and for Pair 3, decide who must be more satisfied with his life. Use your knowledge and understanding of people as you discuss your opinion with your group. Together, try very hard to reach an agreement. Be prepared to tell the class your group's decision and your main reasons for the decision.

Accountability: Have one member of each group give his or her group's decision about one of the pairs.

MODALS: MUST / HAVE TO (OBLIGATION)

Theme: Occupations and responsibilities (Imagination)

Group Size: Whole class (individuals circulating)

Goal: Guess the job pinned on one's back.

Materials: Scrap paper and a straight pin for each student

1. Write on the blackboard:

   You <u>must</u> be very careful about mistakes.

   You <u>have to</u> write down what someone says.

   SECRETARY

2. Have each student think of a job or profession and write it on a scrap of paper. Encourage the class to be creative and think of unusual professions, if possible.

3. Give a pin to each student, who then should pin his or her scrap of paper (with the job written on it) to the back of another student. That student should not know what job is pinned to his or her back.

4. Give the class the following instructions:

   > Walk around the classroom and look at the job written on the back of each classmate. After you look at each job, tell that person what he or she must do as part of that job. For example, if you see *secretary,* (indicate the blackboard) you might say, *You have to be very careful about mistakes,* or *You must write down what someone says.* Do <u>not</u> be so specific or so clear that the person can easily guess his or her job from your sentence. For example, do <u>not</u> say, *You have to type letters for your boss.* Each person must hear several sentences and put together all of the information in order to guess the job on his or her back.
   >
   > When you think you know what your job is, come and tell me. I will tell you if you are correct.

Accountability: If you yourself participate, you can verify accuracy as the students tell you what <u>you</u> have to do for the job written on <u>your</u> back.

Variation: This activity works well as a competition, in which the first three or so people who successfully guess their professions receive small prizes.

MODALS: MUST / HAVE TO (OBLIGATION)

Theme: Transportation safety and responsibilities (Imagination)

Group Size: Three students

Goal: Decide what people have to do in various transportation situations.

1. Write on the blackboard:

bicyclist	pedestrian	train conductor
motorcyclist	bus driver	pilot
ship captain	truck driver	taxi driver

   A bicyclist has to pay attention to cars.

2. Assign two groups for each category on the blackboard (two groups for *bicyclist,* two groups for *truck driver,* and so forth). Use as many categories as are appropriate for your class.

3. Give each group the following instructions:

   > Discuss what the person in your transportation category must/has to do in order to be safe and responsible when traveling.

4. After the students have discussed this topic for five to ten minutes, combine the two groups with the same topic. For example, put the two *bicyclist* groups together, and the two truck-driver groups together.

5. Divide each combined group into pairs. The partners in each new pair should come from different original groups.

6. Give each pair the following instructions:

   > Tell your new partner what your original group decided about the safety and responsibilities of the person in your transportation category. Be prepared to tell the class something your partner's group thought of that was different from your group's ideas.

Accountability: Have one or two members of each combined group (depending on class size) report on the other group's ideas, based on what he or she learned from the new partner.

MODALS: *SHOULD* (OBLIGATION)

Theme: Appropriate behavior (Real information exchange)

Group Size: Three students

Goal: Find at least three items of disagreement.

1. Draw on the blackboard:

2. With the class, label the various age groups of the people on the blackboard (babies, toddlers, children, teenagers, adults, older people).

> Discuss things that you think people of certain ages <u>should</u> and <u>should not</u> do. When members of your group disagree, give reasons for your opinions and disagreements. Try to find at least three things that your group cannot reach agreement on, and choose one of them to tell the class about in order to get their opinions.

Accountability: Have one member of each group come to the front of the class and take a show of hands to get classmates' opinions on the chosen item of disagreement.

MODALS: *SHOULD* (ADVICE)

Theme: Travel advice (Imagination)

Group Size: Three to five students

Goal: Try to think of a piece of advice that no other group thought of.

1. Write on the blackboard:

SHOULD   an English-speaking country

2. Have students choose an English-speaking country that they know a little about or would like to talk about. If a student has been to an English-speaking country, he or she should choose that one. (You might want to brainstorm the names of English-speaking countries before you start this activity if you feel that your class needs some help in thinking of countries.) After they have made their choices, tell the students to find classmates who chose the same country and form a group with them. Some students may have to change their choices if there are no other students who chose the same country as they did.

3. Give each group the following instructions:

> Discuss advice that you would give someone who was planning to visit the country you have chosen. Talk about some of the things you already know about that country to help you think of ideas about advice. If you are having trouble coming up with any ideas, your group may change to a different country. Your advice can be general for travelers, but it also should include items specific to the country you chose. Use *should* as you present your ideas. If possible, try to think of some unusual advice.

Accountability: Have two members of each group come to the front of the class. One person should write the name of the country on the blackboard, and the other should tell the class one or two pieces of advice that the group thought of. Write any unusual pieces of advice on the blackboard, and vote on the most unusual one at the end of the activity.

Variation: If you are teaching in an English-speaking country, have your students discuss advice that they received before they came to that country. Each group should then choose the best piece of advice (the one that turned out to be most appropriate) from all the suggestions in the group.

MODALS: SHOULD / SHOULD HAVE

Theme: Sinking ship (Imagination)

Group Size: Whole class, then pairs

Goal: Write at least one idea on the blackboard.

1. Put on the blackboard:

Captain

crew

passengers

lifeboats/life jackets

sharks

to sink

2. Ask the class, *What are some of the things the people in the ship on the left should do? Their ship is sinking fast.* (You may want to go over the vocabulary.) Write a few answers on the blackboard.

3. Divide the students into pairs and give them the following instructions:

> Discuss the situation for the ship on the right, and decide what the people on that ship <u>should</u> or <u>should not</u> have done. For example (write on the black-board), *They should have put on life jackets.*
>
> Write at least one sentence on the blackboard; it should be different from any ideas already on the blackboard. Be creative; you do not have to be serious.

Accountability: The students' sentences on the blackboard will verify accuracy. Underline all the correct sentences; then, have the students themselves correct errors in the other sentences.

MODALS: SHOULD HAVE / COULD HAVE

Theme: Past mistakes (Imagination)

Group Size: Pairs, then groups of two pairs each

Goal: Prepare a scenario to tell to a new set of partners.

1. Draw on the blackboard:

2. Tell the students the following scenario:

> This is Mike on the left. He is not very happy because he has a problem. He left his car unlocked when he parked it on the street last night. It was stolen. He has no insurance.
>
> (Write on the blackboard): He <u>should have</u> checked the doors before he left the car.
>
> He <u>could have</u> taken out insurance when he bought the car, but he did not want to spend the extra money!
>
> What are some other things Mike could have or should have done? What are some things he should not have done? (Write the students' answers on the blackboard. Remember, *could not have done* does not work well here because it can have a different meaning.)

3. Give each pair the following instructions:

> This is Sally on the right. What is her problem? Discuss with your partner what you think her problem could be. It should be something that happened to her in the recent past. What are some things she could, should, or should not have done? Take notes, but you do not need to write out your sentences. Prepare this little story about Sally to tell to a new set of partners when you are done.

Accountability: Have each pair of students double up with a different pair and explain their scenario about Sally to the new pair. While these new double groups are talking, ask one of them to write their scenarios on the blackboard instead of sharing them orally. Go over these two written scenarios with the class and correct them after all the groups have presented their scenarios to each other.

MODALS: MAY HAVE / MIGHT HAVE / COULD HAVE

Theme: Homeless people (Imagination)

Group Size: Three to five students

Goal: Prepare two or three possible reasons for the situation and write one of them on the blackboard.

1. Put on the blackboard:

PAST POSSIBILITIES

(GUESSING ABOUT THE PAST)

$$\left.\begin{array}{l} \text{may have} \\ \text{might have} \\ \text{could have} \end{array}\right\} + \text{past participle}$$

2. Tell the students the following story:

> This is Brian. He lives on the streets of New York City. He was born and grew up in a beautiful suburb of Chicago. He went to college and had a good job for many years. But now he is fifty years old—poor, jobless, and homeless. What happened?

3. Give each group the following instructions:

> Discuss what may have happened in Brian's life that put him into this position. Use *may have, might have,* or *could have,* followed by the past participle, as in this example: *He might have lost his job in New York.*
>
> Try to come up with two or three reasons and write your most dramatic or exciting one on the blackboard.

Accountability: The students' sentences on the blackboard will verify accuracy. If the students write negative sentences and happen to use *could,* be prepared to remind them that *could not have* expresses past impossibility or inability, but cannot be used for past inference. *He might not have found a job* (past inference) does not have the same meaning as *He could not have found a job* (past impossibility).

REPORTED SPEECH

Theme: Personal questions and answers (Real information exchange)

Group Size: Whole class, then three students

Goal: Report one student's answer to another student.

1. Put on the blackboard:

$$T \xrightarrow[\text{Ask}]{?} A \qquad A \xrightarrow[\text{Answer}]{\text{Whisper}} B \qquad B \xrightarrow[\text{Answer}]{\text{Report}} C$$

(Optional: tense changes for reported speech when the reporting verb is in the past)

2. Call a student to the front of the room. Tell him or her that you are going to ask a question, but that you do not want him or her to answer the question until after you leave the room. When you are gone, the student should answer the questions for the whole class to hear, then call you back into the room. When you are back in the room, call on any student to report back to you the original student's answer.

   Repeat this procedure with about ten questions, such as the following:

What are you going to do tomorrow?	Are you hungry?
Where did you buy those shoes?	Do you like chocolate?
How long have you lived in _____?	Can you swim?
What do you do after school every day?	How many brothers and sisters do you have?
Did you eat breakfast today?	Will you do homework tonight?

3. Give each group the following instructions and indicate the diagram on the blackboard during the explanation:

   > Each group has three students: Student A, Student B, and Student C. I will ask Student A a question. Student A should whisper his or her answer to Student B. Student B should then tell Student C what Student A's answer was.

4. Ask about ten more questions. (The whole-class activity should have been sufficient model for students to do the activity easily.) Your questions can be simple variations of the ones in step 2, such as, *What are you doing next weekend?* or *Where did you buy your pen?*

Accountability: Ask for a volunteer to report to you after each question.

REPORTED SPEECH (IMPERATIVES)

Theme: Simple drawings (Real information exchange)

Group Size: Three students

Goal: Student C will show Student A a drawing for verification.

Materials: Scrap paper for each group

1. Put on the blackboard:

Teacher draws a circle on the blackboard.

Student A: "Tell John to draw a circle."

Student B: "Draw a circle."

Student C (John) draws the circle.

2. Arrange three students and their chairs in the front of the room according to the diagram on the blackboard, with Student A on one end facing the teacher and Students B and C facing away, toward the back of the room.

3. Draw a circle on the blackboard: O Point to Student A (and the model sentence on the blackboard). Tell Student A to say this sentence to Student B. Tell Student B to tell Student C what to do. If Student B needs more coaching, have him or her turn around to see the example on the blackboard. Tell Student C to do what Student B said to do.

   Draw a dot in the middle of the circle: ⊙ Direct Student A to give instructions to Student B as before: *Tell John to put a dot in the middle of circle.* Student B should in turn direct Student C, as before. You might want to add another feature or two to your picture to get the pattern of the activity clear: ∅

4. Give each group the following instructions (after you have arranged the students in the lines of three very carefully):

   > I am going to draw some more pictures on the blackboard, one small part at a time. Student A will watch me and then will tell Student B to tell Student C what to do. Student B will give Student C the instructions, and Student C will draw the picture. When the picture is complete, Student C should show it to Student A to check it.

Accountability: Student C's pictures should match what you drew on the blackboard. You may want to rotate the roles of Students A, B, and C within each group so that everyone has an opportunity to watch, tell, draw, and verify.

Suggested Pictures:

REPORTED SPEECH (SUPERLATIVES)

Theme: Recent experiences (Real information exchange)

Group Size: Pairs, then groups of two pairs each

Goal: Tell a new pair of partners about one's original partner.

1. Write on the blackboard:

MOST IMPORTANT

PAST 5 YEARS

MOST INTERESTING

do	buy	learn	eat/drink
see	break	lose	meet

2. Give each pair the following instructions:

> Choose three verbs from the blackboard and ask your partner a question for each verb following these models (write on the blackboard as you say them):
>   What is the most <u>important</u> thing you have <u>learned</u> in the past five years?
>   What is the most <u>interesting</u> thing you have <u>seen</u> in the past five years?
>   Try to remember your partner's answers.

3. Allow about ten minutes for step 2 and then have pairs of students double up to form new groups of four students (two pairs). Give the new groups the following instructions:

> Tell your two new partners about your first partner using reported speech, such as:
>   I asked my partner the most important thing she had done. She said she had flown in a helicopter.

4. Before the new groups begin, write the model sentence from step 3 on the blackboard and ask two students about their original partners for more examples. Write these on the blackboard and leave them there throughout the activity.

Accountability: During the second part of this activity, walk around the room listening for any difficulties and answering questions. As you circulate, take as many new models as you can from the groups' discussions and write them on the blackboard, preferably with errors uncorrected. When the new groups have finished reporting to one another, have the class correct the sentences you have put on the blackboard.

PASSIVE VOICE

Theme: Local problems (Role play)

Group Size: Pairs

Goal: Each reporter must evaluate what the mayor says and choose the appropriate title for the article that he or she is going to write.

1. Write on the blackboard:

    (results of brainstorming—at least ten problems)

    What has been done?   What is being done?   What will be done?

2. Brainstorm with the class some of the various problems in the town, city, or region you are all living in. If your immediate area does not have enough problems, use the next largest unit (county, state, province, or country) that does have enough problems.

3. Give each pair the following instructions:

    > One partner will be the mayor of our city (or governor of our province or other appropriate official and area) and the other partner will be a newspaper reporter. The reporter is writing an article and should interview the mayor about what has been done, what is being done, and what will be done about each of the problems on the blackboard. Ask and answer the questions in the passive voice. (You might want to remind the students here about the use of the passive voice in English by politicians and others to avoid accepting responsibility for things.) For example, you might ask, if you are the reporter, *What has been done about traffic congestion?* Your mayor might answer, *Last year, fines were increased for drivers who block intersections and lanes of traffic.* (Put these models on the blackboard.)

Accountability: Write the titles *Our Wonderful Mayor* and *Our Terrible Mayor* on the blackboard. Have each reporter declare which title he or she is going to use for the article about the mayor and give a few reasons why, using the passive voice. If any reporter seems to be focusing on the mayor's responsibility, help that student change the sentences to the active voice.

PASSIVE VOICE (SIMPLE PAST)

Theme: Where personal objects were made (Real information exchange)

Group Size: Three students

Goal: Find the most "international" person in the group.

1. Write on the blackboard:

    My watch was made in Switzerland.

2. Give each group the following instructions:

    > Tell the other members of your group where each of the items that you are wearing or have with you right now (such as pens, a wallet, clothes, a watch, and so on) was made. Decide which person in your group has items from the largest number of different countries.

Accountability: Have a member of each group tell the class who is the most "international" person in the group (that is, the person whose things were made in the largest number of different countries). The group's representative should also explain where each of the "international" person's items was made.

Variation: If your students are likely to have every item made in the same place—that is, in their own country—have the groups discuss whether the items were made by hand or in a factory, and to keep a total count in each group as a whole (of how many items were made by hand, and how many in factories). At the end of the activity, add up the totals for the whole class in order to find out what percentage of the class' possessions was made by hand, and what percentage was made in factories. If it is extremely likely that a large percentage of items was made by hand, you might further explore this question—by whom?

PASSIVE VOICE (SIMPLE PAST)

Theme: Famous places, structures, and written works (Real information exchange)

Group Size: Whole class (individuals circulating)

Goal: Estimate when a place, structure, or text was created.

Materials: Scrap paper

1. Write on the blackboard:

building	monument	city	book	document
was founded		was built		was written

2. Ask the class to think of a famous building, monument, city, book, or document whose date of creation they do <u>not</u> know. It is very important to make it absolutely clear that the students are <u>not</u> supposed to know when their chosen item was created. (Students are sometimes inclined to choose automatically something they know about, but to do so will defeat the purpose of this activity.)

3. Write an example of a famous place or written work on the blackboard, preferably one whose dates even you are a little unsure of, such as *Sydney, Australia* (or *the Opera House in Sydney, Australia*).

   Ask the class the following question and write it on the blackboard: *When was Sydney, Australia founded?* (or *When was the Sydney Opera House built?*)

   Survey a few students and write their guesses on the blackboard. Add your own guess, take an average of the most likely answers, and write on the blackboard, *Sydney was probably founded around _____.*

4. Give the class the following instructions:

   > Walk around the room asking other students about the item that you thought of. Ask them in what year it was built or founded or written. Write down your classmates' guesses on a scrap of paper. After you get about ten guesses, decide which year you think is probably the closest to the correct one.

Accountability: Have every student report on his or her chosen item following the model on the blackboard, *Sydney was probably founded . . .* Write the items and the suggested dates on the blackboard, and then record it all on paper for the next class. Have the students find out the actual date for their item as homework. In the next class, compare the students' guesses to the actual dates.

Variation: If your students have been introduced to reported speech, you can practice that structure in this activity by using *I think Sydney was founded . . .,* and so on.

SENSE VERBS + PRESENT PARTICIPLE

Theme: Activities in various places (Imagination)

Group Size: Three to five students

Goal: Describe a group of activities through which a location or event can be identified.

Materials: Scrap paper for notes (optional)

1. Write on the blackboard:

parade	party	concert	movie theater
hotel lobby	station	airport	restaurant
hospital	zoo	gymnasium	campground

see	_____ing
smell	(something)
hear	(someone)
feel	

2. Give each group the following instructions:

> Choose one of the events or places on the blackboard, or one of your own, to describe by using sense verbs and present participles. The class will try to guess what event or place your group is describing, so try not to make it too easy or too difficult to guess. For example, if I say (write on the blackboard):
>
> I see people dancing.
>
> I hear music playing.
>
> I see a man pouring champagne into a woman's glass.
>
>   What event do you think I am describing?
>   Prepare at least six sentences to tell your classmates so that they can guess your event or place. Remember to use sense verbs and present participles, but <u>not</u> the name of your event or place!

Accountability: Have two members of each group present their sentences orally to the class for guessing.

SENSE VERBS + PRESENT PARTICIPLE

Theme: Sights, sounds, and smells (Imagination)

Group Size: Whole class, divided in half (individuals circulating)

Goal: Make a complete sentence with a partner and write it on the blackboard.

Materials: Scraps of paper, one per person

1. Write on the blackboard:

   SEE

   HEAR

   SMELL

       A. person or object that does something visible, makes noise, or produces a smell (flag, radio, baby, fire)

       B. verb of action that can be seen, heard, or smelled (burn, bang, wave, cry)

   We heard a dog barking all night.

2. Divide the class in half, one side to be Group A and the other side to be Group B. Ask Group A to choose a person or object that can make a noise, produce a smell, or perform a visible action on its own. Ask Group B to choose a verb that describes an action that can be seen, heard, or smelled. (Refer to the examples on the blackboard.)

3. Give the class the following instructions:

   > Check your word with me; then, walk around the room. Try to find an appropriate partner among the students who wrote a word from the category that is different from yours. With that partner, write a sentence according to the model on the blackboard. In other words, if you wrote an object or person, find a partner with a verb. (If you are in Group A, you need a partner from Group B.) But you must find a partner whose word makes sense with your own. Your sentence can be funny, but it can't be impossible.
   >
   > For example, if your object or person is *teacher*, you could not pair up with a person who has the word *bark*, but you could pair up with a person who has the word *wave*, (*We saw our teacher waving*), or even *cry* (*We saw our teacher crying*). (You may want to write these examples on the blackboard.)
   >
   > Put your sentence on the blackboard; then try to find new partners and make new sentences.

Accountability: Review the sentences on the blackboard and ask the class for new suggestions, making new combinations with the words already used.

PRESENT PARTICIPLES AS ADJECTIVES

Theme: Student positions in class (Real information exchange)

Group Size: Whole class

Goal: Send all the students in front of the room back to their seats by forming correct sentences.

1. Write on the blackboard:

   The student <u>leaning on the desk</u> sits here.

   The student <u>wearing a green shirt</u> sits next to me.

   —where they are standing

   —what they are doing

   —what they are wearing

2. Have six to eight students come to the front of the class and locate themselves in comfortable positions (sitting on the chair, leaning on the desk, standing by the board, and so on).

3. Give the class the following instructions:

   > These students in front of the class cannot go back to their seats until one of you tells them where they sit. But you must not say the actual names of the students in front of the class. You must identify them by using a present participle that describes where they are sitting or standing, what they are doing, or what they are wearing (indicate the blackboard). When a student in front of the class hears a correct sentence about himself or herself, that student may return to his or her seat.

Accountability: The students must create correct sentences in order to get their peers back to their seats. Once all the students have returned to their seats, repeat the activity once or twice with new sets of students in front of the class.

PRESENT PARTICIPLES AS ADJECTIVES

Theme: Family relationships (Imagination)

Group Size: Three to five students

Goal: Create a story about the figures on the blackboard.

Materials: Scrap paper for notes (optional)

1. Draw on the blackboard:

2. These people in the picture on the blackboard have problems. You are going to describe the people and their relationships to one another, as well as what you think their problems are, according to your own imagination.

3. Tell the students the following model story, and have them listen for the present participles that describe each person as you tell it (point to the figures as you speak):

    The man smoking the pipe is married to the woman sitting in the chair. The baby crying behind the woman in the chair is their daughter. The man sitting on the floor and watching TV is the younger brother of the woman standing by the window. The man standing up and the man looking at the TV are brothers. But nobody knows who the boy holding the bear is.

    What is the relationship between the two women? (Get the answer from the class: *sisters-in-law*).

4. Give each group the following instructions:

    > Create your own story about the people on the blackboard. Try to give the people in your story some kind of problem. Also, prepare a question for your classmates at the end of the story to see if they understood. You may use scrap paper for notes.

Accountability: Have one member of each group tell the class its story, and another member ask the class its question. The first group finished can write its story on the blackboard for correction and as a model for the other groups' presentations.

ADJECTIVE CLAUSES

Theme: Students in the class (Real information exchange)

Group Size: Whole class

Goal: Identify students using adjective clauses.

Materials: Name cards (unless students know one another's names)

1. Write on the blackboard:

I am thinking of the student who . . .

2. Seat the class in a large circle so that everyone can see everyone else. If students do not know one another's names, have them put name cards in front of themselves for identification during the guessing part of the activity.

3. Give the class the following instructions:

> One at a time, each of you should describe another student in the class, using an adjective clause to identify that person. Do <u>not</u> mention the person's name in your sentence. Also, try not to look at that person. You want the class to guess who you are talking about.
>
> For example, if I say (write on the blackboard), *I am thinking of the student who always has the right answer,* who am I thinking of? (Use an appropriate example for your class and wait for the class to guess. You may want to add a few more models before beginning the activity, such as *I am thinking of the man who is wearing a green shirt,* or *I am thinking of the student who always sits in the middle of the front row.*)

4. Give the students three or four minutes to think about their sentences before starting.

Accountability: Since the class sits in a circle and each person must speak to the group, accountability is built in. When the students have difficulty or make errors, you can help them and/or write troublesome sentences on the blackboard. Note that with classes of over thirty students, this activity may run long. However, the guessing aspect keeps it lively.

Variation: This activity can also be used for practicing participial phrases, as in, *I am thinking of the student wearing a green shirt.*

ADJECTIVE CLAUSES

Theme: Drawings of people and houses (Real information exchange)

Group Size: Whole class

Goal: Erase all the pictures on the blackboard.

1. Draw on the blackboard:

    (student drawings) +

2. Have each student come up to the blackboard and draw either a house or a person, keeping it simple, but not too simple. Each student will have to identify his or her own picture by using an adjective clause, so there must be some identifying aspect to each picture. Suggest that the students add hats, eyeglasses, chimneys, trees, and so on, to drawings that otherwise may be too simple to identify.

3. Give the class the following instructions:

> Tell me to erase this picture (point to the woman sitting in the chair). Use an adjective clause to identify it. (After a student has correctly asked you to do this, write a model sentence on the blackboard for students to follow, such as *Please erase the woman who is sitting in the chair.*)
>
>   Now, each of you should tell me to erase the picture that you yourself drew. Use an adjective clause with *who, which,* or *that* to let me know which picture to erase.

Accountability: Do not erase any picture unless the request is correctly phrased. You might also have a student do the erasing, in which case both you and the student can monitor accuracy before erasing anything.

    In a large class (over twenty students), you might wish to have the students do their drawings as they enter at the beginning of class in order to stagger the activity and make the blackboard less congested. Alternatively, have the students do their pictures toward the end of a preceding activity as individuals finish, one or a few at a time.

Variation: This activity can also be used for practicing prepositional phrases (*the man with the hat, the house with four windows, the woman in the chair,* and so on).

ADJECTIVE CLAUSES

Theme: Pens and pencils (Real information exchange)

Group Size: Whole class

Goal: Get one's own pencil back by identifying it with an adjective clause.

1. Write on the blackboard:

    My pen is the one   which . . .

    My pencil . . .   that . . .

2. Collect a pen or a pencil from every student. Students who have a pen or pencil that might be *exactly* the same as someone else's should note some very specific identifying mark on it or choose a different instrument. Put the pens and pencils on your desk and spread them out.

3. Give the class the following instructions:

    > If you want your pen or pencil back, you must identify it by using one of the forms suggested on the blackboard.

Accountability: Pens and pencils are not returned unless the students' sentences are correct.

Variation: If you are sure that a large number of the students have another item (erasers or notebooks, for example), you might add it to the group of pens and pencils in order to make it a little easier and faster for the students to identify items.

   You also might want to do the activity in groups of at least five students, with one strong student in each group serving as the one who collects and returns the objects. In this case, all objects should be of the same type (use just pens, for example), in order to justify the need for the identifying adjective clauses.

GERUNDS AFTER CERTAIN VERBS

Theme: Lazy student (Imagination)

Group Size: Five students

Goal: Create a story, giving reasons for a problem.

1. Put on the blackboard:

May not graduate!

verb + verb + *-ing*

avoid

can't stand

can't help

mind/not mind

enjoy

regret

feel like

detest

can't resist

postpone

2. Tell the students the following little story, referring to the picture on the blackboard:

> This is Ben. He is eighteen years old and he should be graduating from high school this year. But his grades are very low and he may not graduate.

3. Give each group the following instructions:

> Choose five verbs from the list on the blackboard to make five sentences that tell Ben's story—why he may not graduate or what kind of person he is. Use gerunds after these verbs. For example, one of your sentences might be, *Ben can't stand studying for tests.*
>
> Each student in your group should memorize one of the sentences to tell the class.

Accountability: Have each group tell its story about Ben, one student saying one sentence at a time.

Variation: If the class is very large, have the first few groups who finish write their sentences on the blackboard for correction.

GERUNDS AFTER CERTAIN VERBS

Theme: Life in a new country (Imagination for EFL/Real information exchange for ESL)

Group Size: Four to five students

Goal: Cover the blackboard with sentences that contain verbs requiring gerunds.

1. Write on the blackboard:

        avoid

        miss

        enjoy

        have trouble   *verb + -ing*

        imagine

        recall

        consider

        practice

        fear

        can't help

They usually <u>can't help comparing</u> the new country with their old one.

Sometimes they <u>consider going back</u> to their old country.

2. Go over the meanings of the verbs on the blackboard before beginning the activity. (The expression *can't help* is frequently misunderstood as meaning *unable to help,* and might be omitted if too troublesome for your class.)

3. Give each group the following instructions:

> Using the verbs on the blackboard and a gerund, discuss what people living in a new country often do, as in the examples. As you come up with ideas, send a member of your group to the blackboard to write down each sentence. However, if you see that there are already two sentences on the blackboard with a verb that you are using, do not write your sentence but go back to your group and create a new sentence.

Accountability: Review the sentences on the blackboard. If any of the verbs are not represented, try to get volunteers from the class to make up sentences for them orally.

GERUNDS AFTER *DON'T MIND* AND *DISLIKE*

Theme: Household chores (Real information exchange)

Group Size: Whole class (individuals circulating)

Goal: Find the perfect roommate—a person with complementary likes and dislikes of household chores.

Materials: Scrap paper for notes

1. Write on the blackboard:

> dislike
>
> +
>
> don't mind   verb + *-ing*

2. Have the students each think of and write down on a piece of paper three chores they dislike doing around the house, and three unpleasant jobs they don't mind doing at home. Remind the students to use gerunds for the verbs related to these chores. Be sure that everyone clearly understands the expression *don't mind*.

3. Write examples that are true for yourself on the blackboard, such as:

DISLIKE	DON'T MIND
ironing	washing windows

Ask a student, *Do you like or dislike ironing? Do you mind washing windows?* Write these models on the blackboard.

Depending on the student's answers, tell the class whether that student would make a good or a bad roommate for you.

4. Give the class the following instructions:

> Walk around the room asking other students how they feel about all the jobs and chores on your list. Use the models on the blackboard to help you make your questions. Try to find the perfect roommate, that is, someone who likes doing the jobs you don't like and who doesn't like doing the jobs you don't mind doing.

Accountability: Have the "perfect roommates" stand and identify themselves, telling the class how each of them feels about one job on their lists.

CAUSATIVES (HAVE SOMEONE DO SOMETHING)

Theme: Childhood chores (Real information exchange)

Group Size: Four students

Goal: Divide the group into partners, depending on whose parents were most similar.

1. Write on the blackboard:

My father always had me shovel the driveway when I was a child.

(Revise this example according to your own experience)

CHORES   have someone (do) something

DUTIES   (verb in simple form)

RESPONSIBILITIES

2. Give each group the following instructions:

> Discuss things that your parents had (or have) you do—all the chores, jobs, duties, and responsibilities you had (or have) as a child (or teenager). Decide which member of your group has the most similarities with you.

Accountability: Have partners in each group identify themselves and tell the class about at least one similarity in what their parents had (or have) them do.

Variation: With a more advanced class or one which is studying other causative verbs, you might want to expand the choice to include *make* and, for privileges as well as duties, *let*.

Further discussion about the relative virtue of demanding versus lenient parents can lead out of this activity. Projections about the students' own futures (or current situations)—will they be (or are they) demanding parents, and will they give (or do they give) their children more or fewer responsibilities than they had (have)—can also be added for a discussion requiring the extensive use of causatives.

CAUSATIVES (HAVE SOMETHING DONE)

Theme: Having things done for you (Real information exchange)

Group Size: Three to five students

Goal: Agree on something that no one in the group would ever have done for himself or herself.

1. Put on the blackboard:

(+ results of brainstorming)

2. Have the class brainstorm things that people tend to have other people do for them rather than doing for themselves. List the ideas on the blackboard in the causative form *to have something done*, such as:

have one's nails manicured

have one's hair dyed

have the oil changed

have the windows washed

have a tooth filled

Try to get a few unusual or extravagant examples to give the students some ideas about things they perhaps would never consider having done, such as:

have dinner sent up in a hotel

have my nose shortened

have my car driven by a chauffeur

3. Give each group the following instructions:

> Discuss things that you do and do not have done for you. For example, some of you may cut your own hair. Others may have your hair cut. Some of you may repair your car or your bicycle yourself. Others may have it done by a mechanic. Try to find at least <u>one</u> thing that everyone in your group agrees that you would <u>never</u> have done for you—that is, something that you will always do yourselves, or that is so expensive or unnecessary that you will never have it done. Write your answer or answers on the blackboard.

Accountability: Review the sentences on the blackboard. You may want to give the class a model to follow in order to avoid misunderstanding and to make it easier for them to put their agreement into a correct sentence, such as *Our group will never have our nails manicured.*

COMPARATIVES

Theme: Differences among students (Real information exchange)

Group Size: Whole class (individuals circulating)

Goal: Identify the person named on one's back.

Materials: Two scraps of paper and two straight pins per student

1. Write on the blackboard:

YOUR NAME   ANOTHER STUDENT'S NAME

the same _____ as   _____er than

more / less _____ than

2. Have each student write his or her own name on a scrap of paper and pin it to the front of his or her shirt. (The name should be large enough to read from at least ten feet away. If your students know one another's names, this part is not necessary.) Then, have each student write the name of any other student on another scrap of paper and pin that paper to the back of a third, different student. That third student must not know what name is pinned on his or her back.

3. Give the class the following instructions:

> Each of you is going to try to guess what person's name is pinned on your back. In order to do this, you are going to listen to the comparisons that your classmates make between you and this mystery person.
>
> Move around the room from student to student. Each student you talk to should make a comparison between you and the student whose name appears on your back, such as *You are taller than this person,* or *This person sits closer to the teacher than you.* Each student should give you only one comparison. Use the comparative forms on the blackboard.

4. Before beginning the activity, have a student pin the name of some other student on your back. Then ask the class to compare that student with you, the teacher, so that you can guess whose name is on your back. Write a correct example of each form on the blackboard as ideas are given. During this modeling activity, encourage students <u>not</u> to make very personal comparisons, or comparisons that might make a person feel uncomfortable. (Use yourself as the victim.) Tell the students to compare aspects such as clothing, hair, and position in the classroom, rather than weight, intelligence, and beauty.

Accountability: The best way to ensure accuracy is for you, the teacher, to get another student's name on your back and to participate in the activity. As students learn who is the person named on their back, they should verify it with you. If they are correct, take the paper off their backs.

COMPARATIVES

Theme: Houses (Imagination)

Group Size: Pairs, then groups of two pairs each

Goal: Choose one of two houses to buy.

Materials: Scrap paper for each student

1. Write on the blackboard:

ADJ + ER	1.	A number from 6 to 10
MORE	2.	An amount of money between $80,000 and $200,000 (or whatever would
LESS		be appropriate prices for houses in your area)
FEWER	3.	A number from 5 to 100
	4.	A number from 1 to 75
	5.	A number from 0 to 4
	6.	A number from 0 to 12

2. Have the students number from 1 to 6 on a scrap of paper. One at a time, give the students commands to respond to according to the information on the blackboard; the students should write their answers on their scrap papers. In other words, beginning with item 1 (as on the blackboard), tell them to write a number from 6 to 10. For item 2, have them write an amount between your two given figures. Continue this procedure through item 6.

3. After the students have written their numbers on their papers, tell them the meaning of the numbers and write this information on the blackboard as you go:

    1. Number of rooms
    2. Price
    3. Age (in years)
    4. Miles from the center of the nearest city
    5. Number of bathrooms
    6. Number of trees on the property

4. Give each pair the following instructions:

    > Each of you has information about a house that is for sale. Compare your house with your partner's, using comparative forms, and decide which one is the better house to buy.

Accountability: Have each pair join another pair and tell them which house they would buy, using comparative forms to explain their reasons. Then, have one member of each pair write the results of the other pair's decision (in their group) on the blackboard, with a comparison explaining one of the reasons, such as *John's house is bigger.*

COMPARATIVES (ADJECTIVES AND NOUNS)

Theme: Similarities and differences among students (Real information exchange)

Group Size: Whole class

Goal: Get the class to guess "X," the secret student.

Materials: Large scrap of paper for each student (about 1/3 sheet)

1. Write on the blackboard:

    "X" = secret student

SAME	DIFFERENT
↓	↓

    "X" is taller than <u>Jorge</u>.

    "X" is wearing the same color shoes as <u>Ping</u>.

    "X" has longer hair than <u>Olga</u>.

    "X" has more pencils on the desk than <u>Tesfai</u>.

2. If students do not know one another's names, have them make name cards with letters large enough to be visible by everyone in a large circle.

3. Arrange the class in a large circle so that every student can see every other student. Ask each student to place the name card on his or her desk, facing the rest of the class.

4. Ask each student to choose <u>one</u> other student in the class to write about. Emphasize that he or she must choose only <u>one</u> student, and must not tell anyone else which student he or she has chosen. The secret student selected will be called "X."

5. Give the class the following instructions:

    > Write five sentences about your "X." In each sentence, you should compare your "X" with one other student in the class. (Make sure that the students understand that each sentence about "X" should compare "X" with a different student.) In other words, you will write about "X" five times, comparing him or her with five other students, one at a time. (Show the models on the blackboard. After the students begin, walk around the circle to see that they have understood the directions clearly.) Please avoid sentences about baldness and fatness, or anything else that might make a person feel bad or embarrassed. Feel free to make your sentences funny, however.

Accountability: One at a time, have each student read his or her five sentences for the class to guess who "X" is. This activity is a lot of fun, but may run long if your class is large.

COMPARATIVES (ADVERBS)

Theme: A better world (Imagination)

Group Size: Three to five students

Goal: Write as many verbs with comparative adverbs on the blackboard as possible.

1. Put on the blackboard:

People should speak <u>more politely</u> on the telephone.

People should drive <u>less aggressively</u>.

2. Give each group the following instructions:

> Brainstorm ways in which people could change their behavior to make the world a better, more pleasant place to live in. Choose action verbs and add *-ly* to your adjectives to make them adverbs.
>
> Write your ideas on the blackboard, but not in complete sentences. Just write the verb, the comparative word, and the adverb, as in *drive less aggressively*, or *speak more politely*. (Write these examples on the blackboard.)

Accountability: Review accuracy on the blackboard. Then have the class vote on which of the ideas are the three most likely to happen, and which are the three least possible ones.

Variation: For classes who may not have the vocabulary to do this activity easily, you might want to suggest a few verbs and adverbs on the blackboard:

work/play	carefully/carelessly
write/speak	dangerously/safely
spend/use	generously/selfishly
give/take	dishonestly/honestly
drink/eat	neatly/sloppily
help/fix	loudly/softly

COMPARATIVES (ADVERBS)

Theme: Everyday actions and how they are done (Pantomime)

Group Size: Whole class

Goal: Guess the manner in which two students are doing a specific action; then compare them.

1. Write on the blackboard:

quietly	politely	quickly
secretly	slowly	gently
noisily	carefully	carelessly
sleepily	energetically	nervously

2. Have two students come to the front of the class. Tell the class that you are going to have the two students pretend to eat some soup in one of the ways written on the blackboard. Whisper to the two students to pantomime this action slowly. As the two students are "eating their soup," ask the class to guess which adverb (from the blackboard) you told them, and to compare the way they are eating using that adverb. (To make this model clearer, tell the two students who are pantomiming to "eat" <u>very</u> slowly.)

    Write the student-generated comparative sentence on the blackboard, such as, *Sol is eating more slowly than Ting.*

3. Give the class the following instructions:

    > Two students at a time will come to the front of the class and secretly choose one of the adverbs on the blackboard. I will tell them what to do, and they will perform that action in the manner of the adverb they have chosen. The rest of the class should watch them and try to guess the adverb, and then make a comparison—using that adverb—between the way the two students are performing the action.

4. Suggest the following actions to successive pairs of students, and add ideas of your own:

open something (briefcase, a gift)	mix a pot of soup
carry or hold a baby/lay it down	pour something
walk (backwards)	eat a piece of pizza
take off a hat and bow	comb or brush hair
pass money to someone	brush teeth
carry a full cup of coffee	sit down or stand up

Accountability: As this is a whole-class activity, the accountability is built in. To reinforce the comparative form, write a few of the students' answers on the blackboard.

SUPERLATIVES (ADJECTIVES)

Theme: Personal experiences (Real information exchange)

Group Size: Four to five students

Goal: Prepare to tell the class about the most extreme experience of anyone in the group.

1. Write on the blackboard:

UNCOMFORTABLE BED	sleep in
LONG FLIGHT (OR TRAIN OR BUS RIDE)	take
OLD PERSON	meet
FAMOUS PERSON	meet
BEAUTIFUL PLACE	see

2. Give each group the following instructions:

> Tell one another about the most uncomfortable bed you have ever slept in, the longest ride you have ever taken, the oldest person you have ever met, the most famous person you have ever met, and the most beautiful place you have ever seen, as noted on the blackboard.
>
> After everyone has described his or her experience, decide which member of your group had the most extreme experience—that is, which person in your group slept in the worst bed, took the longest ride, and so on. Be prepared to tell the class about that experience.

Accountability: Have one member of each group tell about one of the extreme experiences in that group. After each story, find out if any other group in the class has an even more extreme example of the experience. For example, if one group says that the longest trip in that group was 28 hours on a train, find out if any other group had a longer trip. This way, you can identify the most extreme experiences in the entire class.

SUPERLATIVES (ADJECTIVES)

Theme: Strange, amusing, or embarrassing situations (Real information exchange)

Group Size: Whole class (individuals circulating)

Goal: Write a superlative sentence about a most unusual experience on the blackboard.

Materials: Scrap paper to write out the original question (optional)

1. Write on the blackboard:

   What's the _____est _____ you've ever _____?

   What's the most _____ _____ you've ever _____?

2. Have each student think of a question that fits one of the models on the blackboard. It should be a question that he or she would enjoy asking the other members of the class, and it should be as interesting or amusing as possible. For example (write on the blackboard):

   What's the <u>strangest thing</u> you've ever eaten?

   What's <u>the most embarrassing thing</u> you've ever said?

   What's <u>the oldest vehicle</u> you've ever driven?

3. Give the class the following instructions:

   > Walk around the room asking your question to the other students. Every time you hear a funny, amusing, or interesting answer, write it on the blackboard, such as (write on the blackboard), *The most boring party Tan has ever gone to was . . .*

Accountability: Review the sentences on the blackboard.

SUPERLATIVES (COUNT / NON-COUNT NOUNS)

Theme: Household items (Real information exchange)

Group Size: Whole class (individuals circulating)

Goal: Find out who in the class has the most of certain objects at home.

1. Write on the blackboard:

   one count noun

   one non-count noun

2. Have students think of two items that they are sure everyone in the class has at home. One of these items should be a count noun, and the other a non-count noun.

3. Choose two objects of your own with which to demonstrate the task for the class. For example, using *radios* and *sugar* as your models, write the two words on the blackboard. Then ask four or five students the following questions, writing them on the blackboard:

   How many radios do you have?

   How much sugar do you have?

   Figure out which of the four or five students you questioned has the most of each item, and write sample superlative sentences on the blackboard, such as:

   Kim has <u>the most radios</u>.

   Ilya has <u>the most sugar</u>.

4. Give the class the following instructions:

   > Walk around the room asking one another questions, using *How much?* and *How many?*, about each of your items. You want to find out which person in the class has the most or the largest quantity of each of your items. As you walk around, keep track of the person who has the largest amount of each item.

Accountability: When all the students have had time to talk to at least eight to ten classmates, have each student report his/her findings orally and/or on the blackboard. Examining the content of these sentences could lead to some interesting observations about the students' lives and habits. Gender differences might also lead to some discussion.

SUPERLATIVES (ADVERBS)

Theme: People working together (Imagination)

Group Size: Four students

Goal: Each member must memorize one superlative sentence.

1. Put on the blackboard:

    musicians

    athletes

    office mates

    restaurant workers

Milan types <u>the most accurately</u>.

Tim plays the guitar <u>the most beautifully</u>.

Liu runs <u>the fastest</u>.

2. Give each group the following instructions:

> Choose a situation for these four people (indicate the blackboard) to work together in. It could be a sports team, a musical group, or people working together in any specific job situation. Choose only one job situation.
>
> Decide what each person on the blackboard does the best of anyone in that group or team. Use action verbs and adverbs as you describe each person. Remember that every person in the group is the best at doing one certain thing on the job or on the team.
>
> For example, if you choose a zoo for your job situation, you might say (point to the figures on the blackboard):
>
> Olga feeds the animals <u>the most carefully</u>.
> Tat Ho cleans the cages <u>the most thoroughly</u>.
> Sam hurts the animals <u>the least</u> when giving them a bath.
> Maris gets in and out of the lion cages <u>the fastest</u>.

Accountability: Have each group present its scenario, pointing to the figure on the blackboard, with each member of the group presenting one sentence.

SUPERLATIVES (ADVERBS)

Theme: Simple actions (Real information exchange)

Group Size: Whole class

Goal: Describe the actions of students, using superlatives and adverbs.

Materials: Something to throw, such as an eraser, a piece of chalk, or a ball of paper

1. Write on the blackboard:

read		SLOW	FAST/QUICK
dance		SOFT	LOUD
throw	(most)	CAREFUL	CLEAR
catch	(least)	GOOD	CARELESS
drop		OFTEN	ACCURATE
draw		COMPLETE	NEAT
erase			
write			

2. Have three students who are good readers come to the front of the room with their text-books. Ask each student in turn to read the same two sentences from the book. To take some of the pressure off of the students, refer to them as Student A, Student B, and Student C.

3. Ask the class to make a sentence describing how the three students read, comparing them with one another by using a superlative. Get the class started with a sample that you write on the blackboard, such as *Student B read the most clearly,* or *Student C read the least softly.* Write the class's superlative sentences on the blackboard.

4. Give the class the following instructions:

> I will call different groups of three students to the front of the room to perform the actions written on the blackboard in the left column. In the superlative form, describe the actions of each group, using adverbs from the blackboard, or others that you may think of.

Accountability: As a whole-class activity, accountability is built in. You may want to write some of the students' answers on the blackboard.

CAUSE AND EFFECT EXPRESSIONS:
TOO + ADJECTIVE + *TO*

Theme: Unpleasant edibles (Real information exchange)

Group Size: Three to five students

Goal: Find three or four items that everyone in the group avoids eating, and be
                    prepared to tell the class why.

1. Write on the blackboard:

    TOO
    {
    sour
    spicy (hot)
    messy
    smelly (strange or bad)
    difficult (too much trouble)
    stringy/tough
    salty
    }
    TO EAT

    TO ENJOY

    Lemons are <u>too sour</u> to eat.

2. Go over any new vocabulary and the sample sentence on the blackboard.

3. Give each group the following instructions:

    > Tell some of the things that you do not normally eat because they are too sour,
    > salty, difficult, and so forth, to enjoy. Try to use all the adjectives on the black-
    > board and agree on items that none of you eats for the same reason. Use the
    > expressions too _____ to eat or too _____ to enjoy. (Point to the
    > sample sentence and the adjectives on the blackboard for filling in the blanks.)

Accountability: Have a member of each group reveal its opinions to the class using the
                    correct form. You might want to list the various adjective categories on the
                    blackboard, putting individual items underneath as the students mention
                    them, for example:

SOUR	BITTER	MESSY	DIFFICULT
berries	grapefruit	ripe peaches	pomegranates
plums	parsley	watermelon	nuts in their shells

CAUSE AND EFFECT EXPRESSIONS:
SO + ADJECTIVE + THAT

Theme: Trips and events (Imagination)

Group Size: Pairs

Goal: Prepare a sentence from which the class will guess a place or event.

1. Write on the blackboard:

movie	art museum	concert	play
opera	science museum	parade	party
castle/palace	trip	game	church/temple/mosque

It was *so big that* we couldn't finish it in one day.

2. Give each pair the following instructions:

> Choose one of the events or places on the blackboard and think up a sentence to describe it, using the form *so _____ that*. Do not name the place or event in your sentence. Just use *it* as the subject, because the class is going to try to guess what the place or event is based on your sentence. For example, what do you think *it* refers to in the sentence on the blackboard? (Answer: a museum) Here are a few more examples to guess:
>
> It was <u>so boring that</u> we left at intermission. (play or opera)
>
> It was <u>so interesting that</u> we watched it a second time. (movie)
>
> It was <u>so exciting that</u> the crowd ran onto the field at the end. (game)
>
> When you complete your sentence, write it on the blackboard.

Accountability: Go over all the sentences on the blackboard to correct the grammar and to guess the place or event.

CAUSE AND EFFECT EXPRESSIONS:
TOO + ADJECTIVE + *TO* AND / OR
SO + ADJECTIVE + *THAT*

Theme: Personal problems (Imagination)

Group Size: Three students

Goal: Agree on and memorize a description of a person. Draw the person on the blackboard.

Materials: Scrap paper to practice drawing (optional)

1. Put on the blackboard:

angry	old	tall	full (of food)/stuffed
tired	young	short	poor
weak	thin	hungry	broke
shy	fat	thirsty	stingy

. . . <u>too tall to</u> be comfortable on the school bus

. . . <u>too young to</u> drive

. . . <u>too far to</u> walk

2. Tell the class the following story:

> This is Paul. He is fourteen years old. He is not very happy right now because he grew very fast last year. He is already 6'3" tall. So, he is too tall to be comfortable on the school bus, but he is too young to drive, and his school is too far away to walk to.

3. Give each group the following instructions:

> Choose some of the adjectives on the blackboard and prepare a description of an imaginary person of your own. Use the expression *too* _____ *to* (or *so* _____ *that*) with each adjective in your description.
>   Memorize your description to tell the class, and be prepared to draw a picture of the character you invent on the blackboard.

Accountability: Have all three members of each group come to the blackboard, one drawing the picture and the other two giving the memorized description. If the class is very large, the first few groups who finish can write their descriptions on the blackboard for correction to save time.

CAUSE AND EFFECT EXPRESSIONS:
SO + ADJECTIVE + THAT AND + SUCH (A) + ADJECTIVE + NOUN + THAT

Theme: Superpeople (Imagination)

Group Size: Three or four students

Goal: Create and memorize at least one sentence per student.

1. Put on the blackboard:

SUPERMAN

He is <u>so strong that</u> he can pick up a truck.

He has <u>such powerful eyes that</u> he can see through a wall.

SUPER WOMAN	SUPER FOOL	SUPER STUDENT	SUPER DOG
SUPER TOURIST	SUPER NEIGHBOR	SUPER LANDLORD	SUPER SPY
SUPER TYPIST	SUPER ATHLETE	SUPER THIEF	SUPER SON/DAUGHTER
SUPER KING/QUEEN	SUPER SINGER	SUPER FARMER	SUPER TEACHER

2. Give each group the following instructions:

> Choose one of the "super" people on the blackboard and prepare a description of all the super things that he or she does, using the forms *so* _____ *that* or *such (a)* _____ _____ *that.* Prepare at least as many sentences as there are people in the group. Each member of the group should memorize one sentence to tell the class.

Accountability: Have each group give its memorized sentences to the class. This can be done as a guessing game if desired, with each group keeping its choice of "super" person a secret and just reporting the sentences to the class, who then guess who the group was talking about.

Variation: Choose as many of the "super" people as you have blackboard space for and write them out at the top of the panels as category headings. Then, rather than having each group choose one specific "super" person, groups will create sentences about any of the "super" people and write them on the blackboard under the appropriate heading, such as:

SUPER TOURIST

He has so much luggage that he can't carry it all.

SUPER SPY

She is so smart she can speak seven languages perfectly.

CAUSE AND EFFECT EXPRESSIONS:
SO + ADVERB + THAT

Theme: Fields and professions (Imagination)

Group Size: Four to five students

Goal: Create sentences generated from a discussion explaining success in various areas.

Materials: Scrap paper (optional)

1. Write on the blackboard (spread out as topic headings):

MUSIC   SPORTS   BUSINESS   MEDICINE   AVIATION

A surgeon must work <u>so carefully that</u> she makes no mistakes.

A pianist must practice <u>so hard that</u> his fingers hurt.

2. Give each group the following instructions:

> Discuss what makes a person successful in any of the various fields on the blackboard. You may discuss more than one field, but only one at a time. As you talk, pay attention to the action verbs you use and make sentences with them similar to the two sentences on the blackboard, that is, using *so* followed by an adverb followed by *that*. (Indicate the examples on the blackboard.)
>
> Each time you create a sentence, write it on the blackboard under the appropriate category heading. Your sentences should be logical, but they may also be amusing.

Accountability: As the students are discussing the topics, they will need help producing correct sentences with this form. They will also discover other ideas that could be expressed by *so* + adjective + *that*, which you may choose to ignore or to add to the activity.

Once the sentences are all on the blackboard, correct them, and, if more than one type has been generated, review the differences. This activity can serve as a good medium for the comparison of adjectives and adverbs in a more complex sentence form.

CAUSE AND EFFECT EXPRESSIONS:
SO + ADVERB + THAT

Theme: Extreme situations (Imagination)

Group Size: Pairs

Goal: Create two cause clauses for the class to match with a result.

Materials: Scrap paper for notes

1. Write on the blackboard:

CAUSE	RESULT
	I called the police.
The canary sang <u>so badly that</u> . . .	I moved to a different apartment.
	I left the room.
The neighbors played their music <u>so loudly that</u> . . .	I almost fell off/out.
	I couldn't hear anything.
People were dancing <u>so wildly that</u> . . .	I took it back to the store where I bought it.

VERB + SO + _____LY + THAT

2. Tell the class to look at the cause and result clauses on the blackboard. Ask them to make possible matches between the causes on the left and the results on the right.

3. Give each pair the following instructions:

> Choose two of the result clauses on the blackboard and think of a cause for each of them, using the same pattern as the cause clauses on the blackboard, that is, using an action verb, *so*, an adverb, and *that*. For example, if you choose the result clause, *I almost fell out*, you might say, *I leaned out the window so far that* . . ..
>
>   Be prepared to read your cause clauses to your classmates for them to guess which result clauses you chose.

Accountability: Have each member of every pair read one of the cause clauses for the class to match with its result.

1838

DATE DUE

#47-0108 Peel Off Pressure Sensitive